TI CHURCHILL

North-West Europe, 1944–45

NEIL GRANT

Bloomsbury Publishing Plc
Kemp House, Chawley Park, Cumnor Hill, Oxford OX2 9PH, UK
29 Earlsfort Terrace, Dublin 2, Ireland
1385 Broadway, 5th Floor, New York, NY 10018, USA
E-mail: info@ospreypublishing.com
www.ospreypublishing.com

OSPREY is a trademark of Osprey Publishing Ltd

First published in Great Britain in 2022

A catalogue record for this book is available from the British Library.

ISBN: PB 9781472843883; eBook 9781472843890;
ePDF 9781472843869; XML 9781472843876

22 23 24 25 26   10 9 8 7 6 5 4 3 2 1

Colour artworks by Richard Chasemore
Maps by Bounford.com
Index by Sandra Shotter
Typeset by PDQ Digital Media Solutions, Bungay, UK
Printed and bound in India by Replika Press Private Ltd.

Imperial War Museums Collections

Many of the photos in this book come from the huge collections of IWM (Imperial War Museums) which cover all aspects of conflict involving Britain and the Commonwealth since the start of the twentieth century. These rich resources are available online to search, browse and buy at www.iwm.org.uk/collections. In addition to Collections Online, you can visit the Visitor Rooms where you can explore over 8 million photographs, thousands of hours of moving images, the largest sound archive of its kind in the world, thousands of diaries and letters written by people in wartime, and a huge reference library. To make an appointment, call (020) 7416 5320, or e-mail mail@iwm.org.uk
Imperial War Museums www.iwm.org.uk

Osprey Publishing supports the Woodland Trust, the UK's leading woodland conservation charity.

To find out more about our authors and books visit **www.ospreypublishing.com**. Here you will find extracts, author interviews, details of forthcoming events and the option to sign up for our newsletter.

Dedication
In memory of Phillip Lane (1969–2020), a good man and a good friend.

A note on measure
Both Imperial and metric measurements have been used in this book.
A conversion table is provided below:
1in. = 2.54cm
1ft = 0.3m
1yd = 0.9m
1 mile = 1.6km
1lb = 0.45kg
1 long ton = 1.02 metric tonnes

1mm = 0.039in.
1cm= 0.39in.
1m = 1.09yd
1km = 0.62 miles
1kg = 2.2lb
1 metric tonne = 0.98 long tons

Front cover, above: A late production Tiger I. (Richard Chasemore)
Front cover, below: A Mk IV Churchill tank with a 6-pdr gun. (Richard Chasemore)

Previous page: The crew of a Tiger of 2.Kompanie, s.SS-Pz.Abt. 101 ride outside their vehicle. (Bundesarchiv, Bild Bild 101I-738-0267-18)

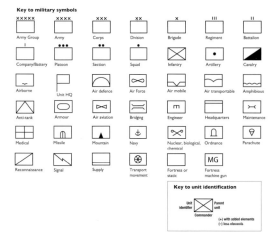

CONTENTS

INTRODUCTION

The Churchill and Tiger are among the most recognizable World War II tanks. Neither was produced in the same numbers as the ubiquitous US M4 Sherman or the Soviet T-34, but when people are asked about famous British and German tanks, they are usually the first mentioned.

The two vehicles' stories contain unexpected similarities. Both were designed hastily in the early years of the war – the Churchill after the British defeat in France in 1940 and the Tiger in response to unexpectedly powerful Soviet armour encountered during Operation *Barbarossa* in 1941 – though both drew on earlier work.

Both had inauspicious combat debuts in the same month, August 1942. For the Churchill, this was the Dieppe raid, intended to seize a French port by seaborne landing. However, the landing forces found themselves pinned down, while the supporting Churchills struggled with the shingle beach before finding engineer teams had not breached the anti-tank obstacles preventing them from moving inland.

The disastrous operation cost 3,600 Allied casualties. All 29 Churchills landed were lost, including several captured almost intact, allowing the Germans to examine the latest British design and parade them for propaganda photographs. The only benefit from the operation was the impetus to develop specialized armour, including the Churchill AVREs used in Normandy.

The Tiger was first used in minor operations near Leningrad. Hitler – eager to see the new tank in action – ordered a platoon to be used in unsuitable marshy and forested terrain, before the crews were used to their new vehicles. The result was predictable: three of the four Tigers involved broke down. A second operation the following month saw more breakdowns while another Tiger bogged in a swamp and had to be destroyed.

Physically, both vehicles had very heavy armour and surprisingly good tactical mobility for their weight, though early versions of both had notable reliability issues.

Both were meant for 'breakthrough' operations to open gaps in enemy defences, but neither had the speed nor strategic mobility to exploit such breakthroughs once created – Churchill units left the dash across France after the Normandy breakout to the faster Shermans and Cromwells, while the Tigers' heavy maintenance and fuel requirements meant they could only be moved any distance by rail.

They also had notable differences. Like most wartime British tanks, Churchills suffered from barely adequate guns, despite several upgrades. By contrast, the Tiger's 88mm was capable of destroying almost any opposing vehicle, though requiring a large and heavy vehicle to carry it.

The two vehicles first met in Tunisia, with mixed results. Churchill crews learned to fear the range and penetration of the Tiger's gun, but equally the first Tiger captured by the British was disabled by a 6-pdr Churchill.

Many books have been written about both tanks. Understandably, they focus on the development and technical characteristics of the vehicles. Tanks do not work in a vacuum, however, and their effectiveness varies with battlefield conditions. Tigers were used very differently on the open steppes of the Eastern Front where they could exploit their 88mm guns' range advantage, compared to the tight Normandy bocage where engagements usually took place at under 1,000m.

Nor do tanks operate in isolation. They work in concert with other units, and depend on support services from ammunition resupply to recovery. An army's ability (or inability) to supply these obviously constrains the effectiveness of the most powerful tank.

Finally, tanks are crewed by men and their levels of skill, training and morale had very significant effects on vehicle performance.

This book will look at the whole picture, and see how these two vehicles worked within the overall Normandy campaign.

A Tiger of 3.Kompanie, s.SS-Pz.Abt. 101 in northern France, spring 1944. The Tigers encountered in Normandy had numerous differences from the vehicles the British first met in Tunisia. The gun travel lock on the rear deck was only installed on vehicles built between November 1943 and February 1944. This particular vehicle was later destroyed during the fighting around Hill 112. (Bundesarchiv, Bild 101I-299-1805-12)

CHRONOLOGY

September 1916   Tanks first used in battle.

June 1919   Treaty of Versailles formally ends World War I and restricts the German military.

January 1933   Hitler becomes chancellor. Existing German rearmament programme accelerates.

September 1939   Britain and France declare war after German invasion of Poland.

May 1940   German invasion of France. British Expeditionary Force evacuated from Dunkirk, losing all its armoured vehicles.

June 1941   Germany invades the Soviet Union. Initial sweeping successes falter, as powerful new Soviet tanks are encountered.

August 1942   Churchill first used at Dieppe, and in North Africa in October. Tiger first used on the Eastern Front, and in Tunisia in December.

April 1943   First Tiger captured by British in Tunisia, knocked out by a Churchill.

June–August 1944   Allied invasion of France, with heavy fighting to break out of Normandy beachheads before the German forces are finally encircled.

August 1944   Tiger production ends.

April–June 1945   Churchills sent to Far East, but none see combat there.

October 1945   Churchill production ends.

October 1950   Churchill Crocodile flame tanks sent to Korea, but used as gun tanks.

1952   Last Churchill gun tanks leave British service, though specialist variants such as bridgelayers and AVREs are retained until 1965.

A Churchill Mk IV of 25th Army Tank Brigade in Italy, May 1944. The Churchill had also evolved significantly from the earlier versions, with new turrets and guns, and would continue evolving into the more heavily armoured Mk VII. (© Imperial War Museum, NA 14891)

DESIGN AND DEVELOPMENT

THE A22 CHURCHILL

Before World War II, the British Army distinguished three types of tanks. Light tanks were used for scouting and 'imperial policing', though they were being replaced by armoured cars. Cruiser tanks were intended for independent 'cavalry' action. They were relatively fast, to outflank and cut off enemy units and exploit breakthroughs, but lightly armoured. Finally, Infantry tanks were relatively slow but well armoured infantry support machines.

The first infantry tank was the two-man machine-gun armed A11 Matilda, followed in 1939 by the four-man 26-ton Matilda II, armed with a 2-pdr anti-tank gun. A third Infantry Tank, the Valentine, did not fit into a logical development sequence, since it was privately developed by Vickers and ordered in July 1939 as the only tank available for immediate production. In September 1939, the army issued a General Staff specification for a fourth infantry tank, the A20.

This reflected fears of World War I-style battlefields re-emerging. It envisaged a vehicle with a long track run to cross wide trenches, ideally with a secondary set of tracks recessed between the main ones for deep mud. A requirement to carry an unditching beam prevented a turret being fitted, so the armament – a pair of 2-pdrs, each with a coaxial Besa machine gun – was carried in World War I-style side sponsons, along with a third Besa in the nose. 80mm armour was specified, proof against the standard German 37mm anti-tank gun.

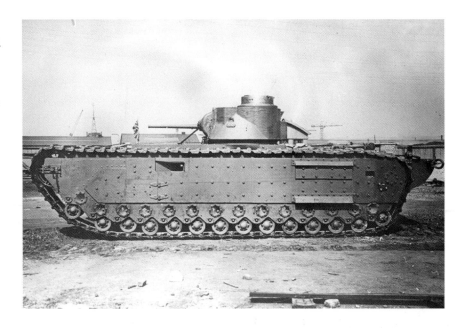

The A20 prototype, fitted with the 2-pdr turret from an A12 Matilda II. The side slots ahead of the turret-mounted additional Besa machine guns. Many design elements, such as the high track run, carried over into the Churchill. (Tank Museum, Bovington)

The Mechanisation Board revised the specification to remove the secondary tracks and unditching beam, putting one 2-pdr into a turret – initially that from the existing A12 Matilda II as a stopgap – and the other in the hull front, though it still included machine-gun mounts in each side. Armour was reduced to 60mm to keep weight down to 32 tons, less than the existing Matilda II's 78mm. A 300hp Meadows DAV flat-12 engine was planned, despite concerns it would be underpowered for the weight, since it was the only one immediately available.

Shipbuilders Harland & Wolff began detailed design work in October 1939, and 100 were ordered in February 1940 without waiting for prototypes. Two mild-steel

A Churchill Mk I of 9 RTR on Salisbury Plain in January 1942, with 3in. howitzer in the hull. The three slots in the cast turret were for the main gun, coaxial MG and sight. Oddly, the coaxial on Mk I and II tanks was on the opposite side of the main gun compared to later marks. (© Imperial War Museum, H 16962)

pilot models were delivered in June 1940, but proved severely underpowered and unreliable, while weight increased to 43 tons, too much for existing bridging equipment. Moreover, the fall of France and the obvious lessons of blitzkrieg rendered the A20 specification irrelevant – the army no longer expected trench warfare in the foreseeable future, and the order was cancelled.

In its place, the army issued specification A22, for a smaller 35-ton vehicle with a more powerful engine and within the 40-ton bridging limit. Vauxhall Motors were appointed as project leaders despite having no previous experience of tank production. Given the dire situation, with fears of imminent invasion, time was short. The Prime Minister wanted 500 of the new vehicle available by 31 March 1941 – only nine months away. Vauxhall completed the design very quickly, and though smaller than the A20 it carried

A Mk II Churchill on a railway flatcar in July 1941. The side air intake louvres (here the early rounded downward-pointing type) would be unbolted and stowed on the rear deck for travel to reduce vehicle width. (© Imperial War Museum, H 11712)

forward many elements of that design, including the long track run, along with 102mm of armour. It mounted a 2-pdr and 7.92mm coaxial Besa in a cast turret, and a 3in. howitzer in the hull front, like the earlier French Char B infantry tank.

The howitzer would fire smoke rounds and high-explosive rounds against infantry positions, against which the small solid 2-pdr armour-piercing (AP) rounds were ineffective. However, its placement low in the hull between the protruding track horns limited traverse and elevation, and thus both range and usefulness of the weapon. Worse, it was loaded and aimed by a single crewman working in a very cramped position, reducing rate of fire. As only a few hundred howitzers were available, it was quickly replaced by a second Besa.

The desperate need to replace tanks lost in France meant that the A22 – technically 'Infantry Tank Mk IV' but named 'Churchill' after the Prime Minister, who took personal interest in it – was pushed straight into production. The first pilot model began trials in December 1940 and tanks started reaching regiments by June 1941. This was impressive, but only achieved by skipping the usual building and testing of prototypes to identify problems.

Unsurprisingly, early production vehicles were plagued by mechanical problems. Vauxhall were unusually frank about this, admitting the faults in the user's handbook but noting they would normally have been identified and resolved during development if not for the urgent need for tanks.

The defects were eventually resolved, but large numbers of vehicles had already been produced. An extensive factory re-work programme was conducted during 1942 with two factories halting new vehicle production to upgrade 700 of the first 1,000 vehicles produced to reasonable standards of reliability; the first 300 were not thought worth updating. Even so, the Churchill was only regarded as a stopgap until better designs arrived.

As tanks were regularly transported by rail, the Churchill's maximum width was set by the narrow British railway loading gauge. This was not merely the distance between

A Churchill Mk III. Note the larger welded 6-pdr turret, newer squarer upward-facing air intakes and track guards to reduce dust. (© Imperial War Museum, KID 810)

rails, but also clearances between track and platforms and height and width limits in tunnels. Since British railway infrastructure was generally older than its continental equivalents, this limited the Churchill to a maximum of 9ft 6in., much tighter than the equivalent German loading gauge of 10ft 6in., even though the track itself was the same.

The high track run inherited from the A20 also meant the turret ring sat between the tracks to keep the centre of gravity low, rather than above them. These factors restricted the Churchill's turret ring to only 54in. (1,350mm), limiting the weapons the turret could mount.

As a result, the Churchill could not be upgraded to carry the powerful 17-pdr, while the Sherman – a smaller vehicle overall, but with a turret ring above its tracks like the Tiger instead of between them – could be developed into the 17-pdr Firefly.

Early marks of Churchill were armed with 2-pdr (40mm) guns, based on the standard British anti-tank gun of the time. This was a good weapon when first developed, but even when the A22 specification was written it was obvious something better was needed, since another 2-pdr tank offered little improvement over the existing Matilda II.

A new 6-pdr (57mm) anti-tank gun was in development. However, almost all existing 2-pdr anti-tank guns had been lost in France and the British concentrated on

The Churchill Mk VI was very similar to the Mk IV, but with a 75mm gun. The commander and loader have separate hatches, while the gunner exited through the commander's hatch. (© Imperial War Museum, KID 4709)

MK IV CHURCHILL WITH 6-PDR GUN

The Churchill NA75 was a Mk IV converted to take the 75mm gun and mantlet of an M4 Sherman. Some 210 were converted in 1944 for service in Italy. The hull Besa was also replaced with a .30 Browning, for ammunition compatibility with the coaxial gun in the new mantlet. (© Imperial War Museum, NA 18530)

replacing these rather than getting newer weapons into production.

This meant the 6-pdr only entered service in May 1942, and until then British tanks in North Africa found their 2-pdrs increasingly ineffective against the up-armoured German tanks they encountered.

Since the Churchill was always intended to carry the 6-pdr when it became available, it might seem sensible to have designed its turret to be upgraded with the larger gun from the outset. Instead, however, the original small cast turret could only take a 2-pdr and had to be replaced by a larger welded plate turret to create the 6-pdr-armed Mk III from February 1942.

Supplies of armour plate suitable for welding proved limited, however, forcing another change to a cast turret for the Mk IV. Alongside new vehicles, existing Mk I and IIs were upgraded to 6-pdr standard by replacing the turrets.

The 6-pdr gave better anti-tank performance, but still had limited high-explosive (HE) capability. Experience in North Africa showed anti-tank positions were actually a greater threat than enemy tanks, and required HE to deal with them effectively. As a result, some Churchills in North Africa were locally modified using 75mm guns and mantlets from damaged Shermans to create the Churchill NA75.

As a more permanent solution, the British 6-pdr was bored out to take American 75mm ammunition. Since these guns had the same external dimensions as the standard 6-pdr, they could be simply swapped out using conversion kits to create 75mm-armed Churchills.

Two vehicles in each squadron HQ troop were armed as Mk V Close Support (CS) variants with 95mm howitzers to deal with hard targets like concrete bunkers rather than tanks.

Churchill production was originally intended to end in March 1943, after 3,500 tanks had been produced. However, the vehicles intended to replace it (most promisingly the A33) offered little advantage over the Churchill now its reliability problems had been resolved and positive performance reports were being received from Tunisia.

Instead of cancellation, the Churchill was redesigned to create the Mk VII, also referred to as the A22F or 'Heavy Churchill'. This featured heavier armour (up to 152mm thick) and a new composite turret with a cast main structure forming front and sides and welded top and

bottom plates. Although even better armoured than the German Tiger, it still carried the same armament as earlier Churchills.

Overall, 5,640 Churchills were built before production ended in October 1945, making it the second most-produced wartime British tank after the Valentine. Although Vauxhall were the lead producer, up to 10 companies produced entire vehicles or major sub-assemblies.

CHURCHILL DEVELOPMENT

Whereas most German wartime tank designs were repeatedly upgraded so they remained viable fighting machines, the British were rarely able to do the same. The Churchill was an honourable exception, and went through 11 marks and numerous specialized derivatives.

The Churchill itself was the 'Infantry Tank Mk IV' producing some rather clumsy nomenclature – a Mk III Churchill was strictly an 'A22 Infantry Tank Mk IV Churchill III'.

Mk I 2-pdr gun and coaxial Besa MG in a small cast turret, with a 3in. howitzer in the hull. A few were built as Close Support versions, with the 2-pdr and howitzer swapped around.

Mk II 3in. howitzer replaced by a second hull Besa.

Mk III 6-pdr and coaxial Besa in a new welded turret.

Mk IV New cast 6-pdr turret but otherwise as the Mk III.

Mk V Close Support variant of the Mk IV, with 95mm howitzer in the same turret.

Mk VI Effectively a Mk IV with 75mm gun. Strictly, only new-built 75mm vehicles are Mk VIs, and those converted are Mk IV (75mm) but functionally identical.

Mk VII An extensive redesign with slightly wider hull, maximum armour thickness increased from 100mm to 152mm, and round rather than square side escape hatches. A new composite cast and welded turret mounted a 75mm gun, and vehicle weight increased to 40 tons.

Mk VIII Close Support version of Mark VII with 95mm howitzer.

Mk IX A conversion of existing Mk III or Mk IV 6-pdr tanks fitted with a Mk VII turret and appliqué armour plates bringing it to Mk VII armour standard.

Mk X Equivalent conversion of existing Mk VI 75mm tank to Mk VII armour standard.

Mk XI Equivalent conversion of existing Mk V 95mm Close Support tank to Mk VII armour standard.

The three 'upgrade' marks were also to be produced as 'Light Turret' (LT) versions, retaining their original turrets. At least 33 Mk Xs were created, but there is little to suggest any Mk IX or XI conversions were actually carried out.

An 'all round vision cupola' replaced the original traversable commander's periscope partway through the Mk VII production run, giving commanders much better situational awareness without exposing their heads.

OPPOSITE

The up-armoured Churchill Mk VII. A welded plate was inserted above the cast sides of the composite turret, and a 'skirt' at the base protected the turret ring. Side escape hatches and the driver's visor were replaced with circular versions, to avoid weaknesses at the corners. (© Imperial War Museum, KID 902)

The exposed tracks of early Churchills kicked up a lot of dust, so track guards were added from the Mk III onward. Crews sometimes removed the centre sections, since they could become packed with mud or even jam the turret if damaged by enemy fire or when crashing through hedges.

Churchills also served as the basis for numerous specialized vehicles, including an unsuccessful tank destroyer – the **Churchill 3in. 20cwt gun carrier** – mounting a high-velocity 3in. anti-aircraft gun in a fixed mount.

The **Churchill Crocodile** was a Mk VII with its hull machine gun replaced by a flame projector with a 120yd range, fed from an armoured 400-gallon fuel trailer towed behind the vehicle. Crocodiles were terrifying psychological weapons, and very effective against bunkers, as the burning fuel penetrated any apertures and consumed all oxygen in enclosed spaces.

A Churchill 3in. gun carrier in March 1943. One hundred were ordered, but this was cut to 50, none of which saw action. Most were converted into other specialized vehicles. (© Imperial War Museum, H 028352)

The **Churchill Armoured Vehicle, Royal Engineers (AVRE)** replaced the standard gun with a short-ranged 290mm 'Petard' Spigot Mortar for destroying bunkers and concrete beach defences. AVREs could also carry a variety of obstacle-breaching equipment, including fascines to fill ditches and 'Bobbins', which laid canvas trackways across patches of soft sand on the invasion beaches. Two squadrons (26 AVREs each) landed in the first wave on each British D-Day beach. Aside from their engineering

A Churchill Crocodile with its armoured fuel trailer, 79th Armoured Division, February 1944. Crocodiles retained their main gun in addition to the flamethrower, and could operate as normal gun tanks. The terror they produced could cut both ways, and there was at least one case of a captured Crocodile crew being executed by the Germans. (© Imperial War Museum, H 35809)

role, they provided valuable fire support for the first infantry units ashore, since the amphibious Sherman DD tanks were delayed by heavy sea conditions and many were lost.

Wartime AVREs were based on Mk III or MK IV hulls, but post-war versions were based on the better-armoured Mk VII and replaced the petard with a 165mm demolition gun, remaining in service until 1965.

The **Churchill Armoured Recovery Vehicle (ARV)** was a turretless version intended to recover damaged tanks for repair and fitted with an A-frame jib to facilitate engine changes. The Mk I version simply carried a repair crew and towed damaged vehicles, while the more capable Mk II had a fixed 'turret' superstructure with a dummy gun containing a 25-ton recovery winch.

Numerous bridge-layers, ramp carriers and other specialized engineering vehicles were also based on the Churchill, but space precludes consideration here.

Table 1: Churchill and Tiger compared		
	Churchill Mk IV	**Tiger**
Crew	5	5
Length	(Hull only) 24ft 5in.	6.3m (hull only), 8.45m (including gun overhang)
Width	9ft 2in. excluding side air louvres, 10ft 8in. including them	3.7m with combat tracks
Height	8ft 2in.	3.0m
Combat weight	39 tons	56 tons
Ground pressure	14lb/sq.in.	1.05kg/cm^2 (14.4lb/sq.in.)
Main gun	Ordnance QF 6-pdr (57mm) Mk V with 87 rounds	8.8cm KwK 36 L/56 with 92 rounds
Gun elevation	+20° to -12.5°	+15° to -8°
Secondary armament	2 x 7.92mm Besa with 7,875 rounds	2 x 7.92mm MG34 with 4,800 rounds
Engine	Bedford Twin-6 (350hp)	Maybach Petrol V-12 HL210 (642hp) or HL 230 (695hp)
Fuel capacity	150 gallons (682 litres)	534 litres
Range (road/cross-country)	127 miles/60 miles	140km/80km
Max speed (road/cross-country)	15.5mph/8mph	40kph/20–25kph
Armour	Hull front 102mm, hull side 76mm, hull rear 51mm, turret front 89mm, turret side and rear 76mm, hull and turret roof 19mm	Hull front 100mm, hull sides and rear 80mm, hull roof 25mm, turret front 100–120mm, turret sides and rear 80mm, turret roof 25 or 40mm
Number produced	5,640 all marks	1,346
Fording depth	3ft 4in.	4.5m early version with snorkel, 1.5m later versions
Trench crossing	10ft 0in.	2.5m

Note: Churchill figures are for the Mk IV; those for the Mk VII would be significantly different, especially in respect of armour, weight and speed.

THE PZKFW VI TIGER

The German Army (Heer) flirted briefly with heavy tanks in 1933–34, with the multi-turreted Neubaufahrzeug ('New construction vehicle') mounting paired 37mm and low-velocity 75mm guns. This was not a success, however, and the three production vehicles were used mostly for propaganda.

The lightweight PzKpfw I and II were really training machines for the panzer arm to build up experience, though both played significant roles in the early blitzkrieg campaigns. After 1937, Germany concentrated on medium tanks in the form of the 15-ton PzKpfw III and 24-ton PzKpfw IV. These emphasized mobility, though both were significantly up-armoured and up-gunned as the war progressed, increasing their weight.

Even so, Henschel & Son received a design contract in January 1937 for a 30-ton Durchbruchswagen (DW), or 'Breakthrough vehicle' to counter French heavy tanks such as the Char 2. It was to be armed with the same short 75mm/L24 gun as the early PzKpfw IV, in a Krupp turret. The DW1 prototype completed in September 1938 carried 50mm armour on hull front, sides and rear. It was made in two pieces and bolted together as the side armour was too long to roll as one piece at that date.

It was followed by the DW2, similar but with automotive improvements and a single-piece hull. One turretless prototype and an armoured hull for ballistic testing were built, before the project was redesignated as the VK30.

Proposals for this VK30 were submitted by Daimler-Benz, Maschinenfabrik

GERMAN TANK NOMENCLATURE

Ironically for the first 'named' German tank, the 'Tiger' designation was originally Porsche's internal designation for their VK4501(P) and only later applied to the whole programme.

German tanks were classified as Panzerkampfwagen (PzKpfw) or 'Armoured Fighting vehicle', followed by Roman numerals. Armoured, tracked or half-track vehicles were also assigned three-digit SdKfz (Sonderkraftfahrzeug, or 'Special purpose vehicle') numbers.

The Tiger was thus PzKpfw VI 'Tiger' SdKfz 181.

Letters indicated particular versions (Ausführung, abbreviated 'Ausf.') with improved guns, armour or suspension. These were originally used alphabetically, but later assigned randomly to confuse Allied intelligence; so the Tiger was the Ausf. H (for Henschel) until March 1943, then Ausf. E.

Experimental vehicles were classified as Versuchs Konstruktion ('Experimental Construction') or 'Vollketten' ('Fully Tracked') depending on which source one prefers, followed by weight class, numerical designator and letter to indicate manufacturer. The VK30.01(P) was thus the first Porsche design for a 30-ton tank.

Tank guns were designated Kampfwagenkanone (KwK), or 'Fighting Vehicle Gun'. Contemporary German sources gave calibre in centimetres, though this book uses the more familiar millimetres. The Tiger's gun was thus the 8.8cm KwK 36.

Guns of the same calibre were distinguished by adding the barrel length in calibres – the Tiger's gun was 493cm long, i.e. 56 x its 88mm calibre, and thus 88mm/L56.

Increasing barrel length increased muzzle velocity, improving range and armour penetration. Thus the 75mm/L24 was a low velocity gun fitted to early PzKpfw IV, the 75mm/L48 was a medium velocity gun fitted to late PzKpfw IV and the 75mm/L70 was a very high-velocity gun fitted to the Panther. Ammunition was not necessarily interchangeable between weapons of the same calibre, since getting maximum benefit from longer barrels required more propellant and thus longer rounds.

Augsburg-Nürnberg (MAN), Porsche and Henschel. The latter two companies were asked to produce four prototypes each of their designs, labelled VK30.01(P) and VK30.01(H) respectively, two for delivery in May 1941 and two in October.

The VK30.01(H) featured 50mm front and side armour, and was powered by a 300hp Maybach HL116 engine. Its body was within the tracks rather than overlapping them – there was no need for them to do so, since it still carried a relatively small Krupp-produced turret for the short 75mm/L24. It did feature an interleaved suspension of the type which became characteristic of the later Tiger, however, with seven wheel stations per side.

By late 1941, the VK30 was obviously under-armed. The turret could be up-gunned with the 50mm/L60 used on the PzKpfw III, but mounting the longer 75mm/L43 used on later PzKpfw IV would require significant re-work.

Meanwhile, the Porsche VK30.01(P) – known internally as the Leopard – used two air-cooled 210hp petrol engines in the rear, driving a generator providing power to separate electric motors for each track. This characteristic Porsche idea greatly simplified steering, since the speed of each track was independently adjustable, but the system suffered significant power losses during transmission. Its suspension was not interleaved.

It was initially intended to carry the same turret as its Henschel equivalent, with the same issues about being under-gunned, but Porsche contracted Krupp to design a larger turret for its VK45, mounting an 88mm/L56 gun, and began to modify the chassis to carry it. This turret would ultimately be used on both Henschel and Porsche Tiger designs. However, the new turret required a 1,850mm (74in.) turret ring, too large for either VK30.

The Porsche VK45.01 (P) during automotive trials, with a dummy turret; the final designs from both Porsche and Henschel used the same turret. Unlike the Henschel design, the track wheels are not interleaved. (Tank Museum, Bovington)

Tiger 131 after its capture in Tunisia, hence the British formation markings. It has the original rubber-rimmed roadwheels, early drum-style commander's cupola, MP port on the rear turret quarter and smoke dischargers. (© Imperial War Museum, STT 4876)

Meanwhile, Henschel also began work on a 36-ton design, the VK36.01, featuring 100mm armour on the hull front, 60mm on the hull sides and 80mm on the turret. It was powered by a 450hp Maybach HL174 engine, and used interleaved suspension similar to the VK30.01(H), but with eight larger diameter roadwheels on each side to cope with the increased weight, which reached 40 tons loaded.

The most radical feature was the turret, mounting the 75mm Waffe 0725 taper bore gun. This fired shells with hard tungsten cores surrounded by compressible soft metal 'skirts' from a barrel whose diameter decreased along its length. By the time rounds exited, they had been compressed down to 55mm and were travelling at very high velocity, giving excellent armour penetration.

A similar weapon was already in limited service as the 75mm/55mm PaK 41 anti-tank gun, but it had several disadvantages as a tank weapon. It could not fire HE rounds and suffered rapid barrel wear. More importantly, it required tungsten for its ammunition, which was in short supply and needed for machine tools. As a result, the Waffe 0725 was abandoned in July 1941.

A replacement turret was ordered from Rheinmetall-Borsig, mounting a long 75mm/L70 high-velocity gun. This was the most powerful weapon that could be fitted onto the VK36.01's 1,650mm turret ring and offered equivalent armour penetration to the 88mm/L56 as higher velocity from the longer barrel offset the lighter projectile. However, this new turret design was not completed before the project was cancelled. One VK36.01 turretless test chassis was completed in March 1942, but the following six pre-production hulls and turrets were never completed.

Meanwhile, the invasion of the Soviet Union saw German forces encounter T-34 and KV-1 tanks, better armed and armoured than their German equivalents.

A German engineering investigation commission reported on a captured T-34 in November 1941. It was not comfortable reading, and within days the existing VK30 and VK36 programmes were cancelled in favour of a heavier tank with much better protection and a gun capable of defeating 100mm of armour at 1,500m, allowing it to destroy Soviet tanks from beyond the effective range of their own guns.

The 30-ton tank programme developed into the VK30.02 programme, with new prototypes from Daimler-Benz and MAN, the latter eventually becoming the PzKpfw V Panther, but that is another story.

The new Soviet tanks were not the sole driver behind the development of the Tiger. Henschel and Porsche had already been asked in May 1941 to develop designs for a new 45-ton heavy tank capable of mounting the 88mm gun and 100mm of frontal armour, intended to enter service in July 1942. It was agreed the new tank would include a submersible fording system, circumventing bridge weight constraints, though it still had to be transportable by rail.

Porsche's submission for this VK45 project was based on an improved and enlarged version of their VK30.01(P) design, featuring the same petrol-electric drive, non-interleaved suspension with six road wheels per side and the Krupp-designed 88mm turret, mounted well forward on the hull. This forward turret position meant the driver and radio operator had no hatches of their own and exited via the turret hatches, making quick bail-outs impossible. It also put too much weight on the leading roadwheels, impairing cross-country performance.

There was a proposal to modify the turret for the new and more powerful 88mm Rheinmetall FlaK 41, but this proved too large. In fact, the FlaK 41 proved troublesome in service and was superseded by the still more powerful Krupp FlaK 43, later fitted on the Tiger II and the Elefant and Jagdpanther tank destroyers.

Henschel meanwhile built two prototypes for the VK45.01(H), based on an enlarged VK36.01(H) with the superstructure extended out over the tracks to accommodate a larger turret ring and fitted with the more powerful Maybach HL210 P45 engine. It used the same interleaved suspension, but with a third roadwheel on alternate wheel stations, allowing wider tracks to spread the extra weight.

The H1 prototype mounted the same Krupp 88mm turret as the Porsche prototype, but positioned more centrally on the hull. A second H2 prototype mounted the 75mm/L70 gun in the smaller Rheinmetall-Borsig turret. This smaller turret, gun and associated ammunition would be significantly lighter than their 88mm equivalents, a weight saving which might have made the Tiger a faster and less maintenance-intensive tank.

It was agreed in March 1942 that only 100 Tigers would be completed with 88mm turrets, and subsequent vehicles would mount the Rheinmetall-Borsig turret with long 75mm. However, this decision was changed in July so all Tigers were completed with the 88mm Krupp turret. The Rheinmetall-Borsig turret and long 75mm were eventually used on the Panther.

Both prototypes were shown to Hitler on his birthday, 20 April 1942. Testing soon proved the Porsche prototype's petrol-electric drive was less than reliable and its suspension was fragile, so the Henschel prototype was selected.

Even allowing for work already done on previous projects, the Tiger's development was notably brief, which inevitably meant it entered service with unresolved issues. More importantly, while the VK45 project set a 45-ton target weight, the final prototype weighed 56 tons, and this extra weight affected both performance and reliability.

The decision to mount the 88mm gun dominated the Tiger design. It effectively determined the size of the turret, since even with the gun mounted as far forward as possible, the breach almost hit the rear turret wall when the gun recoiled after firing.

This in turn set the size of the turret ring at 1,850mm (74in.), so the hull had to be extended out above the tracks to accommodate it, setting the width and height of the vehicle.

The armour was 100mm on the hull front and 120mm on the turret front, enough to defeat most contemporary tank guns except at very close ranges. This forced most enemy tanks to get well inside the range at which the Tiger's 88mm gun would penetrate their armour before their own guns became effective.

The weight of this powerful gun and heavy armour came at a price. Standard Tiger tracks (Marschketten) were 725mm wide, giving the Tiger a fairly reasonable ground pressure of 1.05kg/cm^2 (14.4lb/sq.in.), better than many versions of the US Sherman and very necessary in the snow and mud of the Eastern Front.

However, these made the vehicle too wide for the railway loading gauge, a significant problem since the Tiger's high fuel consumption and short engine life meant rail transport was the only option for moving it any distance.

Crews thus had to go through the back-breaking process of replacing the standard tracks with narrower 520mm Verladeketten – literally 'loading tracks' but commonly referred to as transport tracks – and removing the 16 outer roadwheels before loading their vehicles onto special six-axle s.Syms rail wagons. The standard tracks – weighing 3 tons each – were then rolled and also loaded onto the wagons, as the whole process had to be reversed when the Tigers reached their destination.

The 56-ton Tiger was too heavy for standard German bridging equipment, and for most existing bridges. It was therefore designed to drive submerged across the bottom of rivers up to 4.5m deep. This required a 14-step process to seal every aperture with special plugs, disconnecting the engine fans, starting a bilge pump and erecting a telescopic snorkel to draw in fresh air for the crew and engine while the vehicle was submerged.

The system worked, but was rarely used operationally. Since it added considerable manufacturing complexity, it was only fitted to the first 495 Tigers constructed before August 1943. Later vehicles only had a 1.5m fording capability.

There were numerous changes to the vehicle during its service, including small adjustments like headlight location. Many paralleled changes with other German vehicles, especially the Panther and Tiger II.

The most obvious changes were in July 1943, when the original drum-like commander's cupola with five direct vision slits – which sometimes tore away completely when hit, taking the top half of the commander with it – was replaced with the lower-profile cast version used on the Panther, with its circle of seven periscopes, and the change from rubber-tyred to all-steel roadwheels from vehicle 825 in February 1944.

Triple smoke candle racks were fitted on each side of the turret from August 1942, but discontinued from June 1943 when it was found they could be set off by small-arms fire, potentially incapacitating the crew.

Additional Feifel air cleaners were installed on the rear hull of vehicles intended for 'tropical' countries, including Italy and Southern Russia as well as North Africa and Sicily from November 1942 to August 1943.

Vehicles produced after August 1943 received coats of Zimmerit anti-magnetic paste and external gun travel clamps were added on the engine deck from November 1943.

The original Tiger turret featured two machine-pistol ports in the rear quarters, but the right-hand one was replaced by an escape hatch from turret 46 in December 1942, and that on the left was replaced by a plug from July 1943, then deleted altogether.

From early 1943, Tigers were fitted with five anti-personnel S-mine launchers around the hull for close defence against tank-hunter teams. These were removed from late 1943, replaced by a close defence weapon (Nahverteidigungswaffe) in the turret roof which fired smoke and airburst anti-personnel grenades.

Most Tigers in Normandy were mid or late models, with the new cupola and steel roadwheels.

A total of 1,346 Tigers were built, including 54 using recycled hulls from damaged vehicles. All were assembled at the Henschel factory in Kassel, though many major components came from elsewhere. Turrets were assembled at nearby Wegmann Wagonfabrik, while armour plate came from Krupp and DHHV.

Engines came from Maybach until the plant was bombed by the RAF in April 1944, stopping production until September. Fortunately for Germany, a second production line had almost been completed at Auto Union, and began production in May 1944; without this, there would have been no more engines for the Tiger and Tiger II, or for the Panther and its derivatives, leaving Germany unable to produce any of its more advanced tanks.

Very few Tiger variants were created.

The Tiger captured by the British in Tunisia, with the deep wading snorkel erected. In combination with a process to seal all apertures, this allowed Tigers to ford water up to 4.5m deep, as they were too heavy for most bridges. However, the snorkel was only fitted to the first 495 Tigers built before August 1943 to simplify manufacture. (Tank Museum, Bovington)

LATE PRODUCTION TIGER I

Two Tigers in each battalion HQ were completed as Panzerbefehlswagen command tanks. These replaced the coaxial machine-gun, 1,500 MG rounds and 26 88mm rounds with additional radios, with the loader acting as a second radio operator.

The Sturmtiger (Sturmmörserwagen 606/4 mit 38cm RW 61) replaced the turret with a fixed 150mm armoured superstructure mounting a breach-loading 380mm rocket-launcher. Eighteen were built on reconditioned Tiger chassis, but saw limited use.

A supposed 'recovery variant' was actually a one-off conversion of a battle-damaged vehicle in Italy; its boom winch was too light for recovery work, and was probably intended to place demolition charges.

The 68-ton Tiger II was a completely new design, not a development of the Tiger, with a new and more powerful 88mm/L71 Kwk 43 gun and a new turret and hull with extensively sloped armour up to 150mm thick. Only the engine was the same HL230 unit, so the new heavier vehicle was even more underpowered than the original.

THE STRATEGIC SITUATION

By 1944, German forces had been pushed out of North Africa, but the Allied invasion of Italy proved a slow, grinding advance against multiple deep defensive lines. In the East, the Germans were taking terrible losses, but their situation was not yet irrecoverable and Stalin was pressing the Western Allies for a second front.

Despite commitments in the East, Hitler's 'Fortress Europe' was still strongly held. Allied planners knew that while the initial landings would be a major operation, the real problem would be repelling the inevitable German counter-attacks trying to push the attackers back into the sea, then breaking out of the beachheads.

Aside from assembling the invasion force and finding ways to deliver and support it across the Channel, preparation for D-Day included three key elements.

First was sustained air offensives that attacked German industry and effectively destroyed the Luftwaffe in the West, ensuring Allied air superiority over Normandy.

Second was air attack and sabotage of rail and road infrastructure across northern France, preventing or delaying German supplies and reinforcements reaching the front.

Third was extensive deception plans, convincing the Germans the invasion would come via the obvious Pas-de-Calais route, rather than Normandy. These succeeded so well that the Germans kept forces in the Pas-de-Calais rather than sending them to Normandy well after D-Day, still believing the landings might be diversions from the main attack.

The French coast was guarded by static coastal divisions of second-rate troops with indifferent equipment. These units were expected to fight from fixed defences since

they lacked transport and could only buy time for the German reserves to deploy. It would be these well-equipped panzer divisions (totalling around 1,600 tanks and assault guns) which would then destroy the Allied beachheads.

The placement and control of German reserves was thus critical. Rommel (commanding Army Group B defending the Atlantic coast), based on his experience in North Africa, wanted the reserves well forward, as he believed Allied air superiority would prevent them moving forward if they were far inland, and wanted them under local (i.e. his) control since he believed counter-attacks must be launched early, before the Allies reinforced their bridgeheads.

Meanwhile, Geyr von Schweppenburg (commanding Panzergruppe West), based on his experience on the Eastern Front, wanted the reserves held back from the front and under strategic (i.e. his) control to be committed at the decisive point once the situation was clear.

Characteristically, the confused Nazi command structure then produced a disastrous compromise, splitting control of reserves between the two men so neither had adequate resources to implement his plan, while reserving the final decision for Hitler himself.

The initial landings on 6 June were successful, with lower casualties than forecast. However, they failed to achieve the ambitious breakout plan, which had Caen (14km inland) potentially being reached by the evening of D-Day itself.

Caen was a road and rail hub, and marked the change from the orchards, sunken lanes and dense banked hedgerows of the bocage to more open, rolling countryside. The latter was considered 'good tank country' which would allow the Allies best use of their armour, and it was there, rather than in the bocage, that most fighting was expected.

The original plan was ambitious and relied both on the beach landings going largely to plan, and the Germans not being able to mount significant counter-attacks on D-Day itself. In fact, delays clearing paths through the minefields to get off the beaches and traffic congestion slowed British exploitation, and while the weak and uncoordinated counter-attack by 21st Panzer Division was repulsed, these factors combined to prevent the British reaching Caen before nightfall.

In addition to their 290mm Petards, Churchill AVREs had fittings on the sides to carry a variety of obstacle-breaching equipment. Some 180 AVREs were converted for D-Day, with another 574 converted later. (© Imperial War Museum, KID 898)

The 'Bobbin' allowed AVREs to lay a track across soft sand for wheeled vehicles. This version is fitted with extensions to the air intakes and exhausts, allowing it to wade through deep water during the beach landings. Fitting these and waterproofing the hull was a major task for crews during preparations for D-Day. (© Imperial War Museum, H 37411)

This allowed the Germans just enough time to stiffen their defences with any available troops, and what might have been a simple advance on D-Day required a series of assaults against increasingly strong defensive positions over the weeks that followed.

The British expected the German commanders to follow normal doctrine and fall back to conduct a flexible defence beyond the range of Allied naval gunfire, giving up ground while imposing maximum casualties on the Allies. However, Hitler's refusal to allow any retreat forced them to hold fixed defensive lines. Breaking through these was costly for the Allies, but holding them against repeated attacks with massive artillery, air and naval support cost the Germans almost as heavily.

The deception plan made the German command hesitant to commit reserves to Normandy and those they did send reached the front late and shop-worn due to sabotage and Allied air interdiction of roads and railways. The heavy Tiger battalions suffered particularly, having to complete long road marches for which their vehicles were never designed.

Worse, continual British pressure meant the reserve panzer divisions were committed piecemeal to hold existing defensive lines, or for tactical counter-attacks to regain lost ground, rather than concentrated to deliver the coordinated counter-attack necessary to affect the strategic position.

Short of manpower after five years of war, the British preferred to expend ammunition rather than blood, utilizing their massive material advantage to avoid casualties. In practice, the consequent need to coordinate heavy supporting bombardments slowed their advances to a series of methodical set-piece operations, rather than the swift exploitation attacks the armoured divisions were intended for.

This gave the Germans enough time to reconstitute new defensive lines further back to thwart any breakout. Even strategic bombing was used to break through the defences; although this could prove devastating, it lacked accuracy and sometimes dropped short onto Allied troops. Despite this support, British infantry casualties were extremely heavy.

Caen was not completely cleared until 18 July (D+42). Though the British advance has been criticized for lack of drive, they were fighting through terrain that heavily favoured the defence. When German forces counter-attacked to regain lost ground, they found it equally hard to dislodge the British, and took equally heavy casualties.

Whether or not one accepts Montgomery's later assertion that his repeated offensives were not expected to break the German lines, but deliberately planned to make them deploy almost all their armoured reserves against the British and keep pressure off the US forces, that was ultimately the result. By 25 July, eight German panzer divisions plus all three of the independent Tiger battalions were facing the

British and Canadian forces, while only two panzer divisions faced the equally numerous Americans.

After the US breakout in Operation *Cobra* (25–31 July) delivered a right hook to encircle the German forces, Hitler's irrational refusal to permit withdrawal meant large numbers of German troops were cut off in the Falaise pocket, where they were destroyed or captured.

Meanwhile, Hitler's planned Mortain counter-offensive (Operation *Lüttich*) to cut off the American thrust was effectively stillborn; many armoured formations earmarked for it could not be released since they were holding existing lines against renewed British offensives.

With German resistance broken, Allied forces swept east across France faster than the vaunted German blitzkrieg moved in the opposite direction in 1940. Meanwhile, landings in southern France (Operation *Dragoon*, 15 August) prevented the Germans redeploying other forces in France to contain the breakout, while the collapse of the German Army Group Centre during Operation *Bagration* (23 June–19 August) meant the Eastern Front was now unrecoverable, and precluded any troops being sent west.

Advancing Allied forces were slowed more by supply bottlenecks than by the Germans, and almost reached the German border before the Wehrmacht managed to pull together coherent lines of defence in September.

An ambitious Allied attempt to seize the Rhine crossings with airborne forces in Operation *Market-Garden* (17–26 September) and drive into the Ruhr failed, and with winter closing in, the Germans were able to stabilize the front. They launched a final counter-attack in the West through the Ardennes (the 'Battle of the Bulge', 16 December 1944–25 January 1945), but while this last desperate throw caused real consternation, it achieved little more. Though hard fighting remained, the outcome of the war in the West was no longer in doubt after the Allied breakout in Normandy.

A Tiger of 2.Kompanie, s.SS-Pz.Abt. 101. German AFV crews frequently rode outside their vehicles during the long road marches to Normandy, scanning for approaching Allied aircraft. (Bundesarchiv, Bild Bild 101I-738-0267-18)

TECHNICAL SPECIFICATIONS

All tanks inevitably trade off three key factors: firepower, protection and mobility.

FIREPOWER

A tank's effective firepower depended not only on the power and range of its gun, but also on how easily its crew could spot targets, how quickly they could bring weapons to bear, whether they could hit the target and how fast they could get off the next shot, if the first was not decisive.

Gunners in both vehicles had limited fields of view through their telescopic sights, so most targets were spotted by the commander, higher in the vehicle. Both designs incorporated improved commander's cupolas with better all-round vision than earlier models, though many Churchills in Normandy still had older designs.

The Tiger gunner lacked a periscope, while Churchill Mks I–III and VII–XI gunners had movable periscopes to help spot targets as well as telescopic sights. However, the cast turrets of Mks IV–VI did not include gunners' periscopes.

Neither vehicle had a stabilized gun, and both had to halt to fire accurately. Despite their pre-war belief in firing on the move, by 1944 even the British accepted this simply wasted ammunition.

Aside from their main guns, both vehicles mounted two machine guns – Besas for the Churchill, MG-34s for the Tiger – to suppress enemy infantry. One was mounted coaxially alongside the main armament, while the other was mounted in the hull front and fired by the co-driver/radio operator. However, this had a limited arc of fire and was often blocked by hedge banks or when in hull-down defensive positions.

Anti-aircraft machine guns mounted on the commander's hatch were rarely used in Normandy; commanders had to expose themselves to use one and most preferred to 'button up' inside their vehicles until the aircraft departed.

CHURCHILL

The Churchill was initially armed with an Ordnance QF 2-pdr (40mm) gun. ('QF' denoted 'quick firing', a legacy British term covering almost every tank or field artillery weapon then in service.) The 2-pdr was introduced as an infantry anti-tank gun in 1936, but was effectively obsolete by the time the Churchill appeared and proved ineffective against the upgraded German tanks entering service in North Africa.

It was replaced from 1942 by the high-velocity Ordnance QF 6-pdr (57mm) for the fighting in Tunisia and Italy. Early versions mounted the shorter 43-calibre Mk III gun, later replaced by the Mk V, with a longer barrel for higher velocity.

The 6-pdr had decent armour-piercing performance, but the British discovered in the desert that the main threat to tanks was not enemy tanks but anti-tank guns, which were rarely spotted until they fired and were hard to target with AP rounds due to their low profile. Infantry tanks like the Churchill also needed to destroy machine-gun nests holding up the infantry. High-explosive was needed to deal with both of these, but the 6-pdr's relatively small calibre limited its effectiveness firing HE rounds.

The 6-pdr was thus bored out to use 75mm US ammunition, creating the medium-velocity Ordnance QF 75mm. This had notably better HE effect, but the lower velocity reduced AP performance.

Ironically, the Churchill finally gained decent HE capability just in time for Normandy, where the different circumstances put a premium on dealing with German tanks, many of them more heavily armoured than those previously encountered.

The Churchill Mk V and Mk VIII (seen here) Close Support versions mounted the 95mm howitzer, recognizable by its short barrel with distinctive flat-bottomed counterweight. (© Imperial War Museum, STT 7935)

AMMUNITION

6-pdr ammunition

1. Shot, APCBC, Mk 9T. The initial armour-piercing round for the 6-pdr was simple solid shot, which used kinetic energy to punch through armour then ricocheted around inside the hull. Since solid shot might break up on hitting armour plate or skid off if it didn't hit square, it was upgraded to APC by adding a nosecap in September 1942, and to APCBC by adding a ballistic cap in January 1943.
2. Shot, APCR, Mk 1T. The 'Armour-Piercing Composite Rigid' round introduced in October 1943 had a tungsten core inside a light metal outer, which broke away when the round hit the target, while the hard dense core penetrated the armour. It was effectively a halfway house to proper APDS rounds.
3. Shot, APDS, Mk 1T. The 'Armour-Piercing Discarding Sabot'.
4. Shell, HE, Mk 10T. This had only 40 per cent of the explosive charge of its 75mm equivalent, and lacked effectiveness.

75mm ammunition

5. Shot APC M61. This was a kinetic armour-piercing round, though only moderately effective due to the 75mm's lower muzzle velocity. Though described as APC, it was technically an Armour-Piercing, Capped, Ballistic Capped (APCBC) round.
6. Shell HE M48. The standard and effective HE round could be fused for instant detonation ('Superquick') or a very short delay, allowing it to penetrate foliage or light structures before detonating.
7. Shell WP M64 Smoke. This scattered burning white phosphorous particles throughout the target area, creating a smoke screen. It could also set buildings or dry woodland alight.

88mm ammunition

8. Panzergranate (PzGr 39). The primary armour-piercing round used kinetic energy to punch through armour, with a small bursting charge that detonated after penetration. Technically, the PzGr was an APCBC round in Allied terminology. An improved PzGr 40 APCR round had a very hard, dense tungsten core for better penetration, but the few manufactured went to the Eastern Front for use against Soviet heavy tanks.
9. Sprenggranaten (SprGr). This was the HE round intended for use against infantry positions, anti-tank guns and softskin vehicles. It could be time-fused to air burst, but was generally impact-fused. When it detonated, the explosion sent shrapnel 10m ahead and 20m to either side.
10. Hohladung (Gr 39 HL). This hollow-charge High-Explosive Anti-Tank (HEAT) round had a light windshield nose, behind which was an inverted copper cone backed by explosive. On impact, this punched a jet of molten copper through the armour of the opposing tank. It had lower armour penetration at the muzzle than the PzGr 39, and was less accurate, but its penetration depended on the shaped explosive charge rather than kinetic energy, and did not drop off at longer ranges like the PzGr 39. It was also used as a substitute HE round.

As a result, though most Churchills in Normandy carried 75mm guns, some retained the 6-pdr for its superior anti-tank performance, especially with the new Armour-Piercing Discarding Sabot (APDS) rounds. These contained dense tungsten penetrators within a light carrier that split apart at the muzzle (the 'discarding sabot') while the penetrator – much lighter and less affected by air resistance than a conventional round – flew onward. Its very high velocity (roughly 1.5 times that of conventional AP) gave excellent armour penetration, roughly equal to the Sherman Firefly's 17-pdr firing APCBC.

Unfortunately, APDS rounds only appeared in March 1944, and manufacturing difficulties meant very few (perhaps 10 rounds per tank or less) were available in Normandy. Crews had rarely practised with them before battle, which caused problems since their higher velocity gave much flatter trajectories, changing point of aim at longer ranges. Instabilities from sabot separation meant they lost accuracy beyond 500m, and crews struggled to spot the fall of the very small, fast APDS penetrators to correct their aim for subsequent shots.

The proportion of 6-pdrs varied since 75mm guns were issued as conversion kits for unit installation, but one tank per troop was typical.

The Churchill's electrical power traverse took 15 seconds for a full turret rotation at top speed, much faster than the Tiger. With the engine off, the turret could be traversed manually, but more slowly.

Churchills carried 87 rounds of 6-pdr or 75mm, or 84 in marks with armoured ammunition bins. The manual suggested a mix of 28 AP, 23 HE and 36 smoke, but noted this should vary according to circumstance.

Given their infantry support role, 75mm Churchills usually operated with HE rounds loaded for immediate use, which was awkward when enemy tanks suddenly appeared. However, while HE was unlikely to penetrate armour, it could still disable enemy tanks by shattering vision blocks, destroying radio antenna and breaking tracks.

A 2in. bomb thrower in the turret roof allowed crews to lay smoke ahead of the vehicle.

Close Support Churchills armed with the 95mm Howitzer could fire smoke, HE or High-Explosive Anti-Tank (HEAT) rounds capable of penetrating 110mm of armour, though the howitzer's low muzzle velocity meant hitting a moving tank was notably difficult. Each carried 52 rounds (28 HE, 18 smoke, six HEAT) but space precludes discussing them in detail.

TIGER

The Tiger's KwK 36 gun was derived from the 88mm FlaK 36. This was originally an anti-aircraft weapon but used as an anti-tank gun in France and North Africa, where the high velocity required for its rounds to reach altitude quickly also gave it extremely good armour penetration.

It was adapted for the limited space inside a tank turret by adding a large muzzle break, which reduced recoil by around 70 per cent, shortening the recoil path. Firing the gun without this fitted would wreck the recoil system.

Like other tank guns, it was modified for electrical firing (an electric charge passed through a thin wire in the primer, generating heat to detonate the propellant), so percussion-fired anti-aircraft ammunition could not be used without switching primers.

SS crewmen load 88mm rounds. Their size and weight made them awkward to manipulate in the cramped turret interior. (Bundesarchiv, Bild 183-J14931)

The *Tigerfibel* contained so-called Kleeblatt ('Shamrocks') for a variety of enemy tanks, including the Churchill. The central green zone indicated the ranges from which the Churchill's gun could penetrate the sides and rear of the Tiger; the Germans believed its 75mm gun couldn't penetrate the Tiger's frontal armour at any range. Meanwhile, the much larger red zone indicates the range at which the Tiger's gun could penetrate the Churchill's armour. The German text states: 'Don't let the Churchill get into your shamrock'. (Tank Museum, Bovington)

The high velocity that gave the 88mm its excellent penetration also gave it a very flat trajectory, making accurate range estimation less important.

Gunners were expected to achieve first-round hits on stationary targets at 1,200m, and to hit targets moving across their front at 20kph within three rounds at ranges of 800–1,200m. Experienced gunners could usually hit targets to 2,000m within two to three rounds, and engage targets to 3,000m with some chance of success.

While this long range was extremely valuable in some situations – notably engaging British tanks advancing over open ground during Operation *Goodwood* – the short sight lines in the bocage often prevented Tigers making full use of their range advantage.

The Tiger's main weakness was speed of engagement, both because of slow turret rotation and slow reloading.

The hydraulic turret traverse took at least 60 seconds to complete a full rotation, while doing so using the manual back-up required 720 handwheel revolutions.

The long, heavy 88mm rounds were awkward to handle in the cramped turret. British and Soviet trials with captured vehicles found reloading even from the main racks took a rather slow six to nine seconds, and much longer from the inaccessible underfloor stowage.

Tigers carried 92 rounds of ammunition, 64 ready rounds in hull racks above the tracks and the remainder in reserve bins beside the driver or under the turret floor. These were typically split equally between AP and HE, with a small number of HEAT. One commander noted tanks needed to be ready to fire instantly, and should

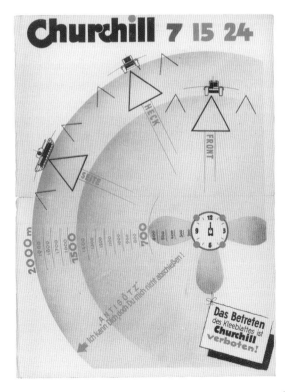

33

keep AP rounds loaded since their flat trajectory covered a wide spread of ranges – with sights set to 800m targets could be engaged from 500 to 1,000m without adjusting aim, and range could be quickly estimated outside those ranges.

PROTECTION

Protection comes from the thickness of a vehicle's armour, and how well it is shaped to deflect projectiles. However, it also includes how likely a vehicle is to survive penetrating hits, rather than catching fire or being immediately destroyed.

AFV crew were hard to replace, and both vehicles had escape hatches, allowing crews to get out without using the exposed turret hatches – crewmen bailing out from damaged vehicles were often machine-gunned. The Churchill had one on each side of the hull usable by any crewmember, while the Tiger had one at the rear of the turret, usable by the three crew there.

CHURCHILL

The original Churchill carried 102mm of armour on the hull front and 89mm on the turret front, the two locations most likely to be struck. This was effectively proof against any German tank gun at normal ranges when introduced, though it became vulnerable as more powerful weapons appeared.

Weight meant the sides and rear obviously carried thinner armour, but still offered reasonable protection at 76mm and 51mm respectively. Despite this, the Churchill had some known weaknesses. In particular, the internal gun mantlet created a shot trap in the turret front, and crews believed its deep shadow gave enemy gunners a clear aiming point. Nor did the Churchill use sloping to increase the effective thickness of its armour or deflect glancing hits, though it was used on tanks entering production at the same time, such as the A13 Covenanter.

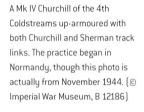

A Mk IV Churchill of the 4th Coldstreams up-armoured with both Churchill and Sherman track links. The practice began in Normandy, though this photo is actually from November 1944. (© Imperial War Museum, B 12186)

Churchill crews landing in Normandy were confident in their vehicles, which certainly offered better protection than other Allied tanks. Indeed, the war diary of 9th Royal Tank Regiment (9 RTR) specifically noted Churchills stood up well to anti-tank fire, were slow to burn and that crews had a good chance of bailing out.

However, combat showed they were not invulnerable and units up-armoured their Churchills by welding on spare track links as extra armour. This may or may not actually have made a difference – the War Office thought it didn't – but it gave crews more confidence.

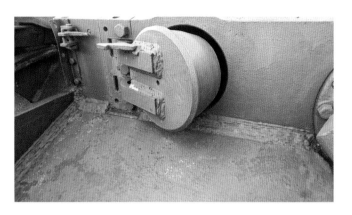

The Churchill Mk VII was up-armoured to 152mm, more than half as much again as the Tiger, as this driver's visor shows. The rectangular driver's visors, Besa machine-gun mounts and side escape hatches of the earlier versions were all replaced by circular designs, to remove weak points at the corners. (Craig Moore)

The Mark VII 'Heavy Churchill' A22F variants appeared from late 1943. This featured 152mm armour on the hull and turret front, and 95mm on the hull and turret sides, though the hull rear remained at 51mm. This was even thicker armour than the Tiger – particularly impressive since the vehicle only gained a ton in weight – and meant crews had a good chance even against 88mm hits.

The greatest risk to tank crewmen was fire, and about 25 per cent of crew casualties were from burns. Most fires were from ammunition rather than fuel, so Mk VIIs gained armoured ammunition bins, which were also retrofitted to some earlier versions. Only a minority of Churchills in Normandy were Mark VIIs, but they became more common as the campaign progressed.

Interestingly, given the powerful tank guns in German service, 21st Army Group operational research concluded that further up-armouring Churchills would have only limited benefits, and that the best way to increase their survivability was actually to increase their firepower: destroying opposing vehicles quicker and at longer ranges would significantly decrease the number of hits the Allied vehicles took in the process.

TIGER

The Tiger was extremely well protected, with 100mm of armour on the hull front, and 120mm on the turret front. Of course, the Tiger's armour could not be equally thick everywhere, but the sides and rear were still a substantial 80mm, giving it an advantage over the Panther, which was very well protected from the front but vulnerable to flank shots.

The lower hull was only 60mm, but was also protected by multiple layers of steel roadwheels. The engine deck and turret roof were only 25mm thick, though concern over air attack and heavy (150mm-plus) artillery shells saw the turret roof increased to 40mm from March 1944.

The armour was assembled using interlocked joints and high quality welding for both maximum structural strength and to waterproof it for submerged river crossings. The armour plates were almost vertical, with even the front plate sloping back at only 81°. By contrast, sloping the armour plates would have increased the chance of deflecting shots away, and increased effective thickness. This could have either increased the Tiger's already impressive protection or allowed it to maintain the same

Tiger hulls in a large jig at the Henschel factory, which aligned them precisely while the turret race was machined into the top plate. The hull sides were milled to receive the final drive casings at the same station. (Bundesarchiv, Bild 101I-635-3965-35)

level of protection with thinner armour, bringing the vehicle back towards its original target weight.

In fairness, the PzKpfw III and IV also featured vertical plates, but both were designed before the war, and it would have been easier to fit sloped armour on the Tiger's welded hull than on the earlier tanks, where the armour bolted together. Meanwhile, the PzKpfw V Panther – designed only slightly after the Tiger – made extensive use of sloped armour.

The Tiger's ammunition was stowed in large unarmoured bins on each side of the hull, which meant rounds penetrating the thick side armour were likely to set it on fire. The engine compartment was sealed for submersion, so any leaking fuel pooled at the bottom, creating a fire hazard, and an automatic engine compartment fire-extinguisher system was fitted to deal with this.

Overall, no Allied tank gun except the 17-pdr or the late-war US 90mm could reliably penetrate the Tiger at decent ranges.

MOBILITY

A tank's weapons are only useful if it can get where they are needed. This involves speed and obstacle crossing, and also how far vehicles can travel without refuelling, servicing or breaking down.

CHURCHILL

One of Britain's main tank design problems was the lack of suitable engines, due to insufficient development in the 1930s and a civilian market that emphasized small lorries not requiring powerful engines. The A12 Matilda II had to use two six-cylinder 7-litre diesel bus engines bolted together. Even so, the combined pair produced only around 170hp, half the 350hp required for the heavier Churchill. Meanwhile, the World War I-era 27-litre V12 Liberty engine used in cruisers such as the Crusader could produce 340hp, but had a notably short life and was too big for the engine bay.

Vauxhall Motors had adopted overhead valve layouts for all their engines in the 1920s, however the new engine needed to be a horizontally opposed side-valve design to minimize its height. A new engine was therefore designed from scratch, in only 89 days from starting work to the first engine on a test bench. The resulting 21.3-litre 350hp twin-six engine used a cast-iron cylinder block and crankcase, cast in two halves with six cylinders each.

Like most British tanks, the gearbox and final drive were at the rear behind the engine. This gave a lower silhouette than US tanks, which generally had gearbox and final drives at the front, requiring a transmission tunnel under the fighting compartment.

The Churchill had protruding track horns to carry the longest possible tracks for maximum trench-crossing ability, a legacy of the A20's focus on trench warfare. However, this also gave a low ground pressure (14lb/sq.in.) so it was less likely to bog down in deep mud. The high incidence angle at which the tracks met obstacles also gave good climbing ability, meeting the GS specification's 5ft obstacle requirement.

The first Churchills had tracks of pressed steel plates with a raised lip, like World War I tanks. These were replaced by the time of the Dieppe raid with tracks of heavy (58lb) cast links, and by Normandy tracks of lighter 48lb cast links were standard. The 11 roadwheels spread the vehicle's weight well, and each was individually mounted on four coil springs, one inside the other.

The front two roadwheels were not in contact with the ground when the tank was on a flat level surface, minimizing friction. The first only came into play when meeting obstacles, and the second only did so on soft ground, effectively increasing track length in contact and reducing ground pressure. Though the suspension on the Mk VII was strengthened for the extra weight, the basic design remained unchanged.

Infantry tanks were never intended to be fast, and the Churchill achieved 15.5mph on roads (12.5mph for the heavier Mk VII) and 8mph cross-country.

Though slow, it had good cross-country mobility, becoming well known for exceptional climbing ability in the mountains of Tunisia and Italy, while later operations in the deep mud of the Reichswald proved it could keep moving through conditions impassable for any other tank.

The Churchill took some practice to drive; the four-speed crash gearbox in particular could be quite tricky. It used Merritt-Browne regenerative steering (ironically similar to that of the Tiger) controlled using handlebars. It could make neutral turns by running the two tracks in opposite directions, allowing it to negotiate the tightest hairpin bends on Italian mountain roads, which Shermans could get round only by backing and reversing several times.

The driver's main problem was visibility. The protruding track horns limited visibility to the side, and while he had a visor for direct vision, this was closed in action, forcing him to rely on his periscopes and instructions from the commander.

TIGER

Like all German tanks, Tigers were fitted with Maybach petrol engines. Initially, this was the 21-litre liquid-cooled V-12 HL210 P45. (HL indicated Hochleistung, or high-performance motor, followed by cubic capacity and P indicating Panzerkampfwageneinbau or tank installation.)

This was a good design, producing 642hp, but had originally been specified for the much lighter VK45, and was severely underpowered in the 56-ton Tiger. It was only used in the first 250 built and replaced from May 1943 by the 23-litre HL230 P45. This produced 695hp, but thanks to better mounting of the auxiliaries it was actually slightly smaller than its predecessor, and could be retrofitted into earlier tanks originally fitted with the HL210 during unit-level engine replacements.

Even with this more powerful engine, the Tiger remained rather underpowered, so the engine was almost always running at maximum output, shortening its life. The HL230 was also used in the 45-ton Panther, where it delivered a much better power-to-weight ratio, but still had maintenance problems.

Tigers of the 'Grossdeutschland' Panzer Division on s.Syms rail cars. They are fitted with the narrower transport tracks and their mudguards have been removed to reduce vehicle width. The crew have pitched a camouflaged shelter-half behind their vehicle. (Bundesarchiv, Bild 101I-732-0133-28)

These problems were made worse by Germany's poor supply situation, which forced use of inferior synthetic rubber seals, hoses and gaskets in the engine. These had rather short lives as they slowly dissolved in the petrol the engine burned and could fail catastrophically at high engine temperatures.

Tiger engines thus had average lives of only 1,000–1,500km, and needed high levels of maintenance and frequent replacement. Fortunately, standardization on Maybach engines meant technicians were familiar with their basic design, and the engine itself was relatively straightforward to remove and replace, provided one had an appropriate crane.

The Maybach Olvar pre-selector gearbox had eight forward gears and four reverse. Though mechanically complex, it was easy to use, and almost universally praised by Tiger drivers.

The Tiger's tracks were driven via front drive sprockets, increasing the vehicle's height, as the turret floor had to be raised above the drive shaft from the engine.

The Tiger's suspension used torsion bars set close together and multiple roadwheels were fitted onto each for a total of 24 roadwheels per side. These extra roadwheels were interleaved to spread the tank's weight, reducing the pressure on each individual roadwheel.

Such interleaved suspensions had been used on several German half-tracks, but no other country adopted them since they had several disadvantages. Mud and ice built up between the roadwheels and froze solid on the Eastern Front, and replacing one damaged roadwheel often meant removing several others to access the damaged one.

Despite this interleaved suspension, the original rubber-tyred roadwheels still broke up too quickly in use. Because of this, and to save scarce rubber, they were replaced by all-steel roadwheels from February 1944. Since these could take higher loads, the outer roadwheels on each side could be deleted, easing replacement.

While the *Tigerfibel* manual was rather optimistic in comparing the Tiger's ride to a sports car, its tactical mobility was actually reasonably good. It had a road speed of 40kph

(25mph) and was capable of 20–25kph (12–16mph) cross-country, albeit using high gear ratios that stressed the engine. This was notably slower than the T-34, which weighed only half as much, but not much slower than the German PzKpfw IV or the US Sherman.

Its wide tracks and interleaved roadwheels spread its weight, so it actually had lower ground pressure than a Sherman – crewmen were advised if they could stand on one leg while carrying a comrade piggyback on a stretch of ground, it would support a Tiger.

Even so, ground reconnaissance and inspection of any bridges was essential before deploying Tigers; schwere Panzerabteilung (s.Pz.Abt.) 503 suffered its first loss of the Normandy campaign even before entering combat, when a Tiger fell through a bridge on the way to the front and was too badly damaged to repair.

While tactical mobility was good, strategic mobility was much poorer – the manual recommended halts for maintenance after the first 5km, then every 10–15km. As a result, road-march speeds averaged 10–15kph by day, or 7–10kph by night, when most German movement in Normandy took place because of Allied aircraft.

The Tiger was actually reasonably easy to drive and far less physically taxing than many tanks of its time. This was due to the Olvar pre-select gearbox and the hydraulic regenerative steering. The latter was the first use of this system – based on the British Merritt-Brown system – on a German tank. It used an automobile-style steering wheel rather than the twin steering levers used on many other tanks. The Tiger was also capable of making a neutral turn in its own length, though this was not recommended on soft ground as it stressed the transmission.

Tracks could also ride up over the sprocket teeth when reversing or turning on boggy ground. If this happened, the immobilized vehicle required two Tigers pulling in tandem to tow it. Worse, the tension on the track prevented it being freed, and the crew had to blow it apart with explosives and replace the broken links with spares.

The driver's biggest problem was poor visibility – his seat was too low for him to see out of his hatch even when not closed up for combat, and he depended on a narrow visor and directions from the commander.

Welding the interleaved roadwheels of a Tiger at the Henschel factory. Without the tracks, the six layers of roadwheels that spread the vehicle's weight can be seen. The change to all-steel roadwheels allowed the outer single layer to be deleted. (Bundesarchiv, Bild 101I-635-3965-28)

THE COMBATANTS

CREW POSITIONS

Both vehicles had five-man crews, with driver and co-driver in the hull and three crewmen in the turret. Crewmen usually received some cross-training, and might change job when promoted or moved between vehicles.

The driver was responsible for most maintenance on the vehicle, as well as driving it. Even the latter required making best use of cover in action, and was hampered because drivers had limited vision when closed down, depending on the commander for guidance.

A hull machine gunner sat next to the driver. Aboard the Tiger, he also acted as radio operator. This was a better arrangement than the Churchill, where the radio was mounted in the turret and operated by the loader, who had other priorities during combat.

The radio combined a short-range set for communication within the troop or platoon and a longer-range set to receive orders from the company commander. Whoever operated it, the fragile valve radios of the period needed constant cosseting, and were easily knocked off the correct frequency by crashing through hedges or the main gun firing.

The noise inside tanks made normal speech almost impossible and each crewmember (except the Tiger's loader) wore an intercom headset connected into the radio.

The turret interior was divided in two by the breech of the main gun, especially as it recoiled into the turret after firing.

The gunner and commander had seats attached to the rotating turret basket, while loaders worked standing, as ammunition bins were spread around the vehicle.

The gunner aimed and fired the main armament and the coaxial machine gun mounted alongside it. The guns were aimed through telescopic sights, incorporating graduations to adjust for range. However, these had narrow fields of view, and gunners were largely dependent on the commander to spot targets. Out of action, the gunner was responsible for maintaining the vehicle's weapons.

The loader's job was to select and load the required ammunition type (AP or HE) as quickly as possible; a quick second shot could mean the difference between life and death if the first missed or failed to penetrate. Out of action, he was responsible for re-stowing the tank's ammunition.

The tank commander was usually a non-commissioned officer (NCO), though one tank in each troop was commanded by the troop's officer. The tank commander picked the best route for the driver, spotted targets for the gunner and integrated his tank tactically into the overall troop plan.

Commanders had the difficult choice of operating with their heads out of the hatches for better visibility and being vulnerable to shrapnel and snipers, or 'closed up', where their limited vision made them vulnerable to infantry tank hunters and concealed anti-tank guns.

Out of action, commanders were responsible for administration and crew discipline.

In heavy action, cordite fumes from the tank's guns built up faster than extractor fans could clear them, and accounts describe air in closed-down vehicles becoming so fume-laden during fierce fighting that crewmen became physically sick, or had to open the hatches to avoid passing out.

BRITISH CHURCHILL CREWS

Britain ended conscription after World War I, keeping only a small professional army. Its tank force suffered particularly badly, as its role in a future war was unclear and little money was available during the 1930s depression.

A Grenadier Guards corporal in RAC helmet, battledress and skeleton webbing with the special low-hung RAC pistol holster. The shoulder braces were supposed to be worn to allow casualties to be pulled up through hatches. In reality, crews avoided anything which might snag while bailing out of a tank, and wore only a pistol belt and holster, often the standard flapped type. (© Imperial War Museum, TR 1410)

CHURCHILL CUTAWAY

Fuel tanks

Commander

Loader

Ammunition racks

Driver

Gunner

Co-driver/hull gunner

JOHN FOTHERGILL, 107 REGT RAC

John Fothergill was born in 1916. He was conscripted into The King's Own Royal Regiment (Lancaster), an infantry battalion converted to tanks in November 1941, and redesignated as 107 Regt RAC. He was selected for officer training, and was a lieutenant commanding a troop when he first saw action after D-Day.

In July 1944, his Mk VII tank 'Briton' and its crew were the subject for an army photographer. The photos were widely published, and are preserved in the Imperial War Museum Collections (IWM B7601–B7645). Fothergill seems to have taken over as squadron commander, presumably as an acting replacement since he was not promoted. He was killed in August 1944 when his tank was penetrated by an 88mm shell.

John Fothergill. (© Imperial War Museum, B 7622)

Limited conscription was reintroduced in May 1939, then extended to all males between 18 and 41 when war broke out in September, though not everyone eligible could be trained immediately and some were not 'called up' for actual military service until 1941.

Men could express preferences for particular services, and the large navy and air force both had higher priority than the army for the more technically minded recruits. Even within the army, tank units had only medium priority for the best recruits. Overall, armoured units made up only 7 per cent of British Army manpower for the Normandy campaign – just ahead of signals (5 per cent) and far less than those assigned as engineers (13 per cent) or artillery (17 per cent).

Pre-war training in the Royal Tank Corps depot at Bovington provided comprehensive instruction in all aspects of armoured warfare. However, this was only possible because so few men were being trained and it had to be drastically simplified to cope with the enormous expansion of British armoured forces during the war.

Initially, men were almost arbitrarily assigned to particular regiments and received their basic and advanced training in that regiment, so infantry regiments trained soldiers as infantrymen. However, this often led to men being used in roles they were poorly suited for, and in 1942 it was replaced by a more scientific system.

Men now received basic training centrally, covering skills common to all soldiers, such as drill, map reading and basic marksmanship. They were then assigned to particular roles based on aptitude testing. Potential tank crewmen went to one of the Royal Armoured Corps (RAC) training regiments, which specialized in particular tank types, to receive training in driving and maintenance, gunnery or signals, depending on their assignment.

The 'All-Round Vision' cupolas were installed on Mk VII Churchills to give the commander better visibility from under armour, and retrofitted to earlier versions. Ahead of it is the vane sight, which allowed the commander to help lay the main gun on target. (Author)

The earlier drum-like Tiger cupola was replaced by this lower profile cast design in July 1943. It featured a circle of periscopes instead of the older vision slots and a commander's hatch that swung sideways rather than upward. The ring welded above the periscope hoods could mount an AA machine gun. The same design was also used on the Panther and Tiger II. (Craig Moore)

Meanwhile, most existing cavalry regiments and even some infantry regiments were converted wholesale into tank units, though this inevitably meant transferring in cadres of tank men, and transferring out existing men who couldn't make the switch.

Training was initially limited by shortages of tanks, ammunition and even space for firing ranges. By D-Day, however, these problems had largely been resolved, though the shortage of tank gunnery ranges meant units only got a few weeks' live firing each year, notably less than their German counterparts.

Overall, British tank crews were reasonably well trained in the technical aspects of their role, and replacements could quickly slot into existing crews. However, only men expected to become tank commanders were given any tactical instruction, causing problems as commanders proved disproportionally likely to become casualties and other crewmen took over as commanders in the field.

The tactical training received was limited and focused at troop or squadron level, with occasional regimental exercises allowing whole units to train together. Shortage of space for training meant few larger-scale exercises took place. The 6th Guards Tank Brigade was only able to conduct one brigade-level exercise (the ten-day Exercise *Blackcock* in September–October 1943) during its entire preparation for D-Day, for example, and few units could practise alongside infantry.

More importantly, almost all British tank units with combat experience from the North African desert were still fighting in Italy, and none of those that did return to the UK were assigned to infantry tanks.

The Churchill regiments therefore landed in Normandy with no actual combat experience. While they would gain this quickly enough, it put them at a notable initial disadvantage compared to their more experienced opponents.

GERMAN TIGER CREWS

The Versailles Treaty after World War I restricted the German Army to a maximum of 100,000 men, outlawed conscription and set minimum enlistment terms of 12 years to prevent the army taking men for short training enlistments to create a large reserve while keeping the active army small.

However, the army command worked to undermine these restrictions even before the Nazis came to power. The long enlistments meant soldiers could be very thoroughly trained to prepare them for promotion as NCOs in an expanded force. Since Germany was prohibited from possessing tanks, a secret tank warfare school was created in the Soviet Union.

Once Hitler gained power, he quickly cast aside the Versailles restrictions. Conscription was

TIGER CUTAWAY

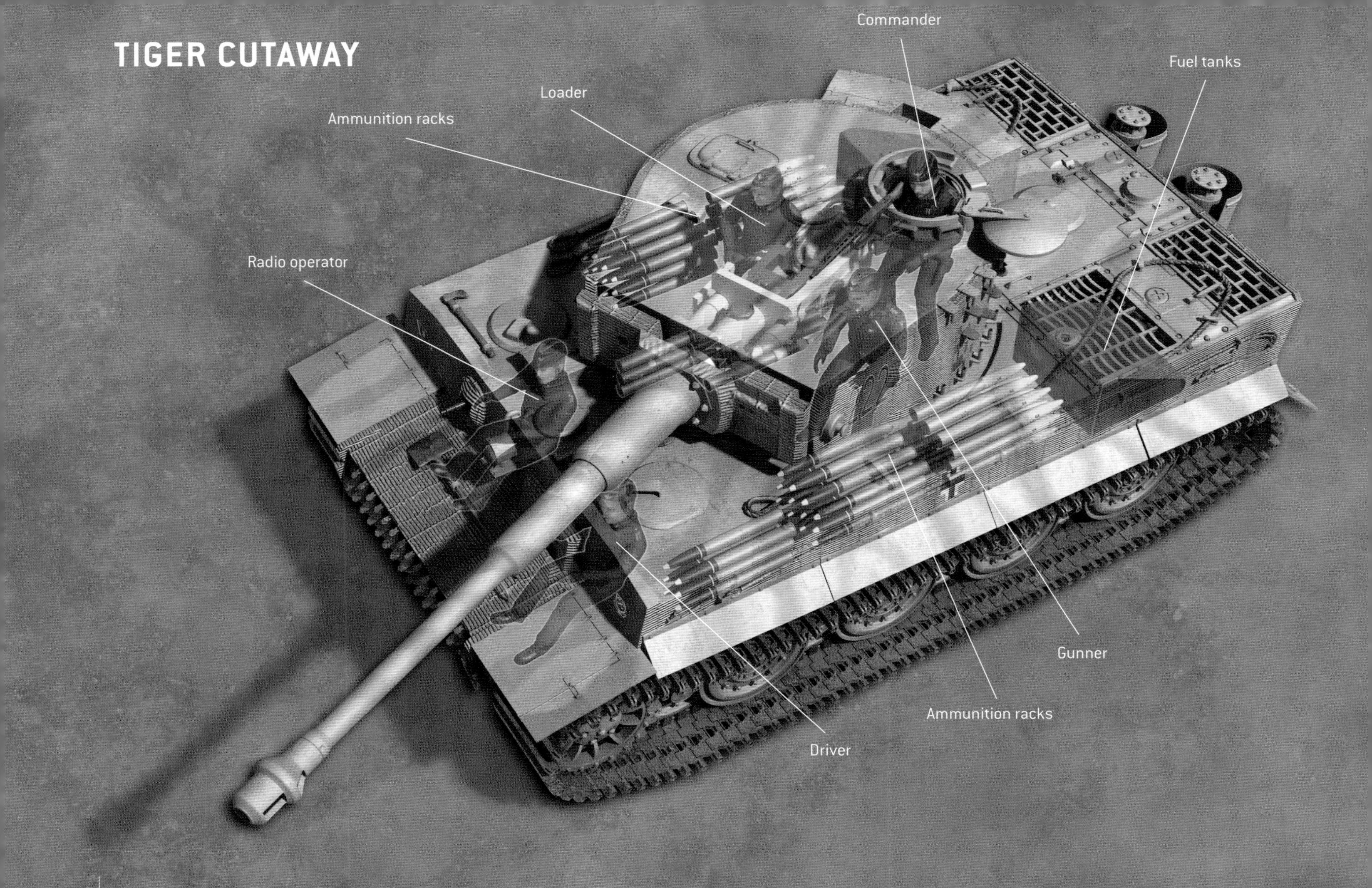

Fuel tanks

Commander

Loader

Ammunition racks

Radio operator

Gunner

Ammunition racks

Driver

RICHARD FREIHERR VON ROSEN, s.PZ.ABT. 503

Richard Freiherr von Rosen was born in 1922 into a minor noble family. He joined the army as a volunteer officer cadet in October 1940, and trained as a tank crewman. He served as a PzKpfw III gunner during the invasion of the Soviet Union in 1941, and was injured when a bridge collapsed under his tank in August 1941. He was sent back to Germany to recover and completed officer training, graduating top of his class. He was assigned to the first unit equipped with the new Tiger tank and commanded a platoon on the Eastern Front. He was wounded again at Kursk in July 1943, returning to duty in June 1944 just as s.Pz.Abt. 503 transferred to France.

Von Rosen's unit lost all their Tigers in Normandy, and the remaining men were transferred to the replacement depot before the encirclement, where they were re-equipped with new Tiger IIs. He was promoted to company commander in September 1944, and sent to Hungary in October. He was lightly wounded, but remained with his unit until severely wounded in February 1945. Evacuation to a military hospital in Bavaria, in the American occupation zone, saved him from capture by the advancing Soviet forces along with the rest of his unit. During the war, von Rosen was awarded the Iron Cross first and second class, and the German Cross in gold. After the war, he served in the German Bundeswehr for 22 years, ending as a major-general commanding an armoured brigade. He died in 2015 aged 93, and his memoirs were published as *Panzer Ace* (von Rosen 2018).

reintroduced for all men aged 18–45 in 1935, and extended to two years in 1936. Before joining the armed forces, men also served six months in the state labour service (Reichsarbeitsdienst, RAD). This provided manpower for road-building projects, agricultural work etc., but also ensured men were used to hard physical work, living in barracks and basic drill before even beginning recruit training.

Even before that, most boys spent years in the Hitler Youth, which was the only youth group permitted in Germany from 1934 and became compulsory from 1936. Alongside organized sports, hiking and fieldcraft, it also provided thorough indoctrination in Nazi ideology and basic paramilitary training.

It even included motorized units, which trained drivers and mechanics for the National Socialist Motor Corps (Nationalsozialistisches Kraftfahrkorps, NSKK, which provided transport for the Nazi party), and for the armed forces.

Once recruits joined the army, they received thorough basic infantry training – though this was shortened somewhat as the war went on – before going on to specialist training. The panzer force featured heavily in German propaganda, and had high priority for the best recruits.

Those selected for panzer training received intensive instruction in their speciality (driver, gunner or wireless operator) and basic cross-training in other crewmembers' jobs to fill them in an emergency. Officer and NCO training was notably thorough, and it was emphasized that even junior NCOs and enlisted men should use their own initiative rather than waiting for orders.

While the panzer force trained with wood and canvas dummies on car chassis in its first years, quality rapidly improved. Early practical experience from the Spanish Civil War and the first blitzkrieg campaigns helped develop the curriculum, and instructors were usually experienced combat veterans.

Given the value of Tigers, their crews were initially specially selected and usually had experience in other tanks before receiving a three-week conversion course. Maintenance personnel and drivers – who bore most of the maintenance burden –

The *Tigerfibel* (*Tiger Primer*) used cartoons, jokes and rhymes to make technical information easy for recruits to absorb and remember. (Tank Museum, Bovington)

were seconded for several weeks to the Henschel factory, so they knew the vehicle from the ground up.

Even manuals were designed to be user-friendly – the *Tigerfibel* (*Tiger Primer*) was filled with cartoons and jokes designed to make technical information easy to remember.

Germany had been at war for five years by 1944, and armoured units usually had combat experience on the Eastern Front before being withdrawn to Germany or occupied Western Europe to re-equip, integrate replacements and rest. While Tiger

Tank commanders of 3.Kompanie, s.SS-Pz.Abt. 101 during exercises in May 1944. Uniforms include both standard and camouflage versions of the Panzer jacket, dispatch riders' coats and leather clothing taken from naval stocks. (Bundesarchiv, Bild 101I-299-1805-03)

A quad 20mm FlaK half-track next to a Tiger in the USSR in spring 1944. The twin holes on the Tiger mantlet are for the binocular TZF 9b sight. (Bundesarchiv, Bild 101I-090-3947-12)

units included a proportion of new replacements, tank commanders and a good percentage of other personnel often had considerable experience, especially since the Germans took care to return wounded men to their original units. Overall, this experience would make a significant difference to combat performance.

The Normandy battles probably represented the last high point of the German armoured forces. After this, catastrophic losses meant Germany had to accept ever-lower-quality conscripts, and training was increasingly abbreviated due to shortages of time, fuel and ammunition.

Although 11 of the 14 Tiger battalions created were army formations, two of the three Tiger battalions which fought in Normandy actually belonged to the Waffen-SS. This originated as the military wing of the Nazi party, and fielded steadily larger military units as a fourth branch of the armed forces from 1939. The original strict physical and racial standards for recruits were relaxed as the war progressed, and they began to accept conscripts and even recruited extensively from conquered territories.

The army were initially reluctant to supply SS units with equipment and vehicles, since it needed all those produced for its own expansion. By 1944, however, political manoeuvring meant the Waffen-SS had a relatively high equipment priority.

SS units have sometimes been mythologized as elite formations. In reality, their training closely resembled the army's, and used the same manuals. SS units did typically operate very aggressively due to ideological indoctrination, but the army believed SS officers were not as thoroughly trained as their army equivalents, and that SS units suffered from a lack of experienced NCOs.

BRITISH ARMY CHURCHILL REGIMENTS

Just as the British Army divided tanks into cruisers and infantry tanks, it had two types of armoured unit. Armoured Divisions were equipped with cruiser tanks or US Shermans, which were intended for manoeuvre and exploitation, and included the support arms necessary to operate independently. Meanwhile, infantry tanks were organised into Army Tank Brigades, each made up of three Infantry Tank Regiments and intended to support infantry divisions. Since they lacked organic infantry or artillery, they could not operate independently.

Each Churchill regiment was commanded by a lieutenant-colonel, with a major as second-in-command, and consisted of a regimental headquarters (RHQ) squadron, plus three sabre squadrons (A, B and C) each commanded by majors, with captains as second-in-command.

The HQ Squadron consisted of:
- RHQ troop (4 x Churchills, 1 x armoured command vehicle);
- Reconnaissance troop (11 x Stuart light tanks);
- Link troop (10 x Dingo or Humber Scout Cars);
- Anti-aircraft troop (6 x Crusader 20mm AA tanks).

Each of the three Sabre Squadrons consisted of:
- Squadron HQ troop (1 x Churchill, 2 x 95mm CS Churchill, 1 x Churchill ARV);
- Five Churchill troops (each with 3 x Churchills).

Eight Churchill Observation Post (OP) tanks with Royal Artillery Forward Observation Officers were attached to each brigade, and usually assigned one per squadron, while three Churchill bridge-layers were held centrally as a brigade resource.

This fighting echelon was supported by an 'A Echelon' of trucks assigned to each squadron, which resupplied the tanks with fuel, ammunition and rations at temporary leaguers near the front lines. It also provided specialist support, including the unit medical officer (with an armoured half-track to evacuate wounded under fire), and the Royal Electrical and Mechanical Engineers (REME) fitters Light Aid Detachment in half-tracks.

The 'B Echelon' only came forward when units were out of the front line and included baggage, the field kitchen and the officers' mess truck.

Tank crewmen might be temporarily rotated to rear-echelon duty to rest after heavy combat, though driving trucks loaded with fuel and ammunition within enemy artillery range was hardly 'restful'.

Each regiment thus had 58 gun or CS tanks, plus 11 light tanks and six AA tanks, and a total of 38 officers and 670 other ranks. For simplicity, the 130-odd wheeled softskin support vehicles have been omitted.

Infantry Tank regiments were often split up – commonly, one squadron supported each of the three battalions of an infantry brigade, with a three-tank troop supporting each infantry company, only reuniting at the unit's leaguer each night. Ideally, tanks should have consistently supported the same infantry units so they learned to work together, but poor British doctrine prevented this.

TREVOR GREENWOOD, 9 RTR

Trevor Greenwood was born in 1908 near Manchester, and prior to World War II worked as an electrical sales engineer. He was 32 and already married when called up in an early batch of British conscripts in late 1940.

Greenwood rose to become a sergeant commanding a Churchill before D-Day. He first saw action in Normandy, including at Hill 112, and served through the rest of the North-West Europe campaign. His military career is typical of many enlisted tank commanders, who would never have joined the peacetime army, but served when called up. After VE Day, he did occupation duties in Germany until 9 RTR was disbanded and he was demobilized in December 1945.

He returned to his old job after the war, having no interest in continuing in the army, and remained there until retirement. He died in 1982 and his edited diaries were published as *D-Day to Victory* (Greenwood 2012).

Trevor Greenwood. (Courtesy Julie Schroder)

Other units might also be attached – a troop of M10 tank destroyers (with 3in. or 17-pdr guns) was often attached to each Churchill squadron, providing anti-tank support as Fireflies did for Sherman units.

This was obviously an idealized organization. Most regiments disbanded their AA troops towards the end of the Normandy campaign in the absence of significant air threats, reassigning the crews as casualty replacements.

Only three of the eight Army Tank Brigades in Normandy were equipped with Churchills:

- 34th Tank Brigade, comprising 147th, 107th and 153rd regiments Royal Armoured Corps (RAC). The first elements landed in Normandy on 16 June 1944 (D+10), though the last elements only arrived in early July.
- 31st Tank Brigade, comprising 7th RTR, 9th RTR and initially 141st Regiment RAC. The latter operated Churchill Crocodiles, and transferred to the 79th Division with other specialized armour almost immediately. The brigade landed in Normandy on 19 June 1944 (D+13).
- 6th Guards Tank Brigade, comprising 4th Bn Grenadier Guards, 4th Bn Coldstream Guards, and 3rd Bn Scots Guards, landed in Normandy on 20 July 1944 (D+44).

In addition, 1st Assault Brigade, Royal Engineers (comprising 5th, 6th and 42nd Assault regiments RE) operated Churchill AVREs, with their first elements landing in the initial waves on D-Day. These specialist vehicles were usually attached in small numbers to other formations, rather than operating together, and are outside the scope of this book.

Churchill mark	6th Guards Tank Brigade	31st Tank Brigade	34th Tank Brigade	Total	Unit reserves
Mk III		60	90	150	
Mk IV	156	19	18	193	49
Mk IV OP	8	8	8	24	
Mk VI		31	24	55	30
Mk VII		45	24	69	44
Mk V or VIII (95mm)	18	18	18	54	15
ARV Mk I	11	11	11	33	5
Bridgelayer	3	1	2	6	
Gun tanks	**174**	**173**	**174**	**521**	**138**
Total Churchill	**196**	**193**	**195**	**584**	**143**
75mm conversion kits	164	41	59	264	122

Table 2: Churchill tanks in Normandy by unit

Notes

Total establishment for all three brigades should have included nine bridgelayers, not six. The reserves were also three bridgelayers and an ARV short, but otherwise at full establishment.

31st Tank Brigade included 141 RAC, and most of its tanks (notably 45 Mk VIIs) were Crocodile flamethrowers.

Kits to convert 6-pdr tanks to 75mm were issued separately.

THE GERMAN TIGER BATTALION

Each Tiger required too many resources and lacked the mobility required for it to become the standard German tank, so the small number available were concentrated in special schwere Panzerabteilungen (s.Pz.Abt.) or Heavy Tank battalions. These were intended as spearhead units for larger conventional formations, smashing gaps through enemy defences that lighter tanks could pour through while the Tigers, with their short endurance, were withdrawn for repair and maintenance. Overall, 11 army and three SS Tiger battalions were formed.

The original Tiger battalions organized in August 1942 contained a HQ company with two Tigers and six PzKpfw IIIs. They were originally planned to have three tank companies, made up of a HQ platoon with a Tiger and two PzKpfw IIIs, plus four platoons with two Tigers and two PzKpfw IIIs each. However, most units initially had only two tank companies, for a total of 20 Tigers and 26 PzKpfw IIIs.

The lighter and more mobile PzKpfw IIIs were intended to act as scouts and flank security, allowing the few Tigers available to be deployed where they would have most effect.

In March 1943, Tiger battalions were reorganized to replace the PzKpfw IIIs with Tigers, and structured as a HQ Company (Stabskompanie), plus three Heavy Tank companies (schwere Panzerkompanien, numbered 1–3) and a Workshop company (Workstattkompanie).

The HQ Company consisted of:

- HQ platoon (3 x Tiger, 1 x SdKfz 251 light half-track);
- Armoured Reconnaissance platoon (7 x SdKfz 250 or 251 light half-tracks);
- Scout platoon (Kettenkrad, Schwimmwagen and Kubelwagen);
- Engineer platoon (3 x SdKfz 251/7 light half-tracks);
- Anti-Aircraft platoon (usually 3 x SdKfz 7/1 medium half-tracks with quad 20mm, though other vehicles were possible).

Each of the three Heavy Tank companies consisted of:

- Company HQ (2 x Tiger);
- Three Tiger platoons (each with 4 x Tiger);
- Medical and light repair detachments.

The Workshop company consisted of:

- Two Workshop platoons (each with 1 x FAMO SdKfz 9/1 half-track with 6-ton crane);
- Recovery platoon (4 x or later 6 x FAMO SdKfz 9 18-ton half-tracks, 1 x SdKfz 9/1 with 6-ton crane);
- Communications, armourer and quartermaster detachments.

Each battalion thus had 45 Tigers, plus seven Reconnaissance half-tracks and three AA half-tracks, and a total of 34 officers and 845 other ranks. However, the equipment actually available might not match the theoretical organization. For simplicity, the 200 wheeled or tracked softskin support vehicles required to keep the unit supplied and operational have been omitted.

Tiger units were at least fully motorized; even in late 1944, only 16 per cent of German divisions were fully motorized rather than relying to some extent on horse-drawn transport, and even units supposedly equipped with trucks often had far fewer than they should have.

Scout and engineer platoons were necessary since deploying the heavy Tigers usually required careful route selection and often reinforcement of tracks and bridges, while the entire Workshop company shared the maintenance workload to keep the Tigers operational.

The weight of the Tigers required recovery assets to be centralized, as several SdKfz 9 were required to move one Tiger. Along with the specialized equipment in the Workshop company, this meant battalions would struggle to recover and support their Tigers if split up, which is exactly what happened in Normandy.

While the tanks of the Tiger battalion were more powerful than their British equivalents, the reverse applied to almost everything else. The British reconnaissance element had 11 light tanks versus seven half-tracks in the German equivalent, and its anti-aircraft, recovery and medical evacuation vehicles were armoured, whereas the Germans depended on softskin vehicles.

Three Tiger battalions (two SS, one army) fought in the Normandy campaign, though none were immediately available on D-Day:

- schwere SS-Panzerabteilung 101. This had to move from Beauvais and arrived in Normandy on 12 June (D+6). It was renumbered as the 501st in late 1944.

MICHAEL WITTMANN, S.SS-PZ.ABT. 101

Michael Wittmann was born in Bavaria in 1914. He completed his two years' army service as an infantryman from 1934 to 1936, then joined the SS. He took part in the annexation of Austria in 1938 and joined the Nazi Party that year.

On the Eastern Front, he commanded an armoured car, then a StuG III assault gun and finally a PzKpfw III before officer training, becoming a Tiger platoon commander in January 1943. He was awarded the Knight's Cross in January 1944 for high numbers of enemy tank kills, with oak leaves added later that year. He was promoted to company commander when his unit moved west in April 1944.

German propaganda made Wittmann famous for his lone attack near Villers-Bocage on 13 June 1944. Unfortunately, the often-quoted German citation that Wittmann destroyed 25 British tanks is notably inaccurate; he actually destroyed 12, including two unarmed OP tanks and three Stuart light tanks, and 13 half-tracks and carriers.

The British were surprised, with many crews out of their vehicles, and Wittmann's victory should not be taken as proof of the Tiger's superiority. He certainly displayed skill and bravery, and halted a dangerous British advance.

However, he also showed questionable tactical judgement – his rush to attack meant he left his company leaderless for the rest of the day, and he could certainly have accomplished more with even a reduced company than he did alone. Moreover, taking his tank into a built-up area without accompanying infantry – strictly against guidelines – resulted in having to abandon it after being immobilized by a 6-pdr anti-tank gun.

After Wittmann's Tiger was disabled, both understrength companies available from his battalion and a PzKpfw IV company mounted a follow-up attack, and the effects of this are often conflated with Wittmann's solo attack.

Overall, the best estimate is that between the two attacks, the British lost 27 tanks and a similar number of light AFVs, while the Germans lost six Tigers and two PzKpfw IVs.

Wittmann was awarded the Knight's Cross with swords after the action, and promoted to SS-Hauptsturmführer. However, he was killed in action on 8 August 1944, leading a number of Tigers across open ground; five, including Wittmann's, were rapidly destroyed without inflicting any casualties on the enemy.

Michael Wittmann. (Bundesarchiv, Bild 101I-299-1802-08)

- schwere SS-Panzerabteilung 102 was initially moved to the Calais area, then ordered to Normandy on 14 June. It moved by train to Versailles in late June, but still faced a long road march to Normandy, with its first tanks reaching the front on 7 July (D+31). It was renumbered as 502nd in late 1944.
- schwere Panzerabteilung 503 was the only army (rather than SS) Tiger battalion in Normandy. It reached the front on 7 July. It was the only Tiger battalion in

Normandy to have Tiger IIs, with two Tiger I companies (33 tanks) and one Tiger II company (12 tanks).

A single understrength mixed company with three Tiger Is and five Tiger IIs – of which only one Tiger I and two Tiger IIs were operational on 1 June – was also assigned to the Panzer-Lehr-Division.

CAMPAIGN EXPERIENCES

Both British and German tank crewmen in Normandy suffered weather that alternated between choking clouds of dust and pouring rain, and often spent days pinned inside their tanks by mortar or artillery fire, relieving themselves in empty shell cases.

Sleep became precious as long summer days meant fighting continued well into the evening; Churchill units might not be released by the infantry they were supporting until 2230hrs, while Allied air superiority meant Tiger units could only move at night. Once operations ended, tanks met up with their supply echelon in night leaguers and crews began basic maintenance, then refuelled and rearmed their tank for action the next day.

Refuelling and re-arming a Tiger was heavy work, and often had to be done in darkness in Normandy. The stippled surface of the Zimmerit anti-magnetic paste can be seen on the rear hull. (Bundesarchiv, Bild 146-1978-107-06)

One experienced Tiger commander reckoned each hour of operation required ten man-hours of work from the crew, even if no regular service or repair work was required.

A full ammunition load totalled almost a ton of ammunition for a Churchill, or a ton and a half for a Tiger. Refuelling was equally back-breaking – unless a pump was available, it meant lifting 20–30 25kg jerrycans above head height onto the engine deck before pouring them into the fuel tanks.

After the vehicle was fuelled and armed, crewmen might grab perhaps four to five hours of sleep until 'stand to' before dawn, taking turns on sentry duty. Most slept in slit trenches or under their vehicle as a precaution against artillery during the night.

There was rarely time (and often no water) for washing; at best, crews might be able to clean oil from their hands and slept in their dirty uniforms, removing the outer layer and boots.

Tank units included field kitchens in their support echelons, but these were rarely practical in the front line, where units were often split up and heavily engaged. Crews lived mostly on packaged rations, supplemented with food bought from locals.

TIGER-PHOBIA AND JABOSCHRECK

Only 140 Tigers actually fought in Normandy, but they exerted a disproportionate psychological effect. Knocked-out examples were inspected with awe and fear, and every half-seen German tank became a 'Tiger' until proven otherwise. The PzKpfw IV was often misidentified in this way, since the side skirts and spaced armour around the turret changed its appearance notably.

Concerned about the effect on morale, General Montgomery moved quickly to quash any discussion about the superiority of the Tiger and Panther over British tanks, and insisted in public that British tanks were just as good. He expressed serious concerns that British designs were well behind their German counterparts in private, however, and pushed hard for more 17-pdr-armed vehicles.

If British troops suffered from 'Tigerphobia', their German opponents suffered equally from 'Jaboschreck' or fear of Jagdbomber – rocket-armed Typhoons and Thunderbolts which ranged across the battlefield under complete Allied air superiority.

These ground-attack sorties were much less effective than thought at the time – later Allied operational research showed many vehicle kills claimed by aircraft were actually destroyed by their own crews after breaking down or running out of fuel – but they still exerted a major effect on the Germans.

Along with British artillery, with its apparently limitless ammunition, they terrified even veterans of the Eastern Front, where Soviet air power was far less dominant, and Tigers sometimes used smoke candles to simulate being hit when attacked.

This meant German units could only move at night and camouflaged themselves during the day, except when bad weather grounded Allied aircraft – perhaps a third of the campaign – notably delaying reinforcements and supplies reaching the front.

A Tiger crew of s.SS-Pz.Abt. 101 camouflage their vehicle, though they clearly still need to conceal the protruding barrel. Even tread marks were often brushed out in an attempt to avoid Allied air attacks. (Bundesarchiv, Bild 101I-738-0275-09A)

COMBAT

INFANTRY SUPPORT AND COOPERATION

The Churchill was not designed to fight other tanks, but for infantry support. The need for this was painfully apparent in Normandy, when German unwillingness to withdraw out of naval gunfire range forced the British to fight through the tight bocage country, which they had neither expected nor planned for, and where dense terrain prevented outflanking movements.

German infantry dug into the hedgerows were effectively immune to small-arms fire. They could be suppressed by artillery, but re-emerged after the bombardment ended to inflict heavy casualties on the advancing British infantry.

Overall, infantry made up only 15 per cent of 21st Army Group's manpower, but took 70 per cent of the casualties, forcing some units to be disbanded to keep others up to strength. Infantry tanks provided direct fire support to deal with machine-gun nests holding up the infantry and allowing them to advance.

Tank support kept up infantry morale, but they were dangerous to be around, both because their poor visibility meant they could crush infantry who got in their way, and because tanks and the dust they kicked up drew German artillery.

They also provided vital immediate anti-tank support. Infantry battalions had six towed 6-pdrs in an organic anti-tank platoon, but until these guns could be brought forward and dug in, the infantry depended on one short-ranged PIAT (Projector, Infantry, Anti-Tank) per platoon. As German doctrine emphasized immediate counter-attacks to regain lost ground, the extra firepower of the Churchills was essential to holding any ground taken.

Finally, tanks brought forward extra ammunition and water and even carried the infantry themselves on long operations.

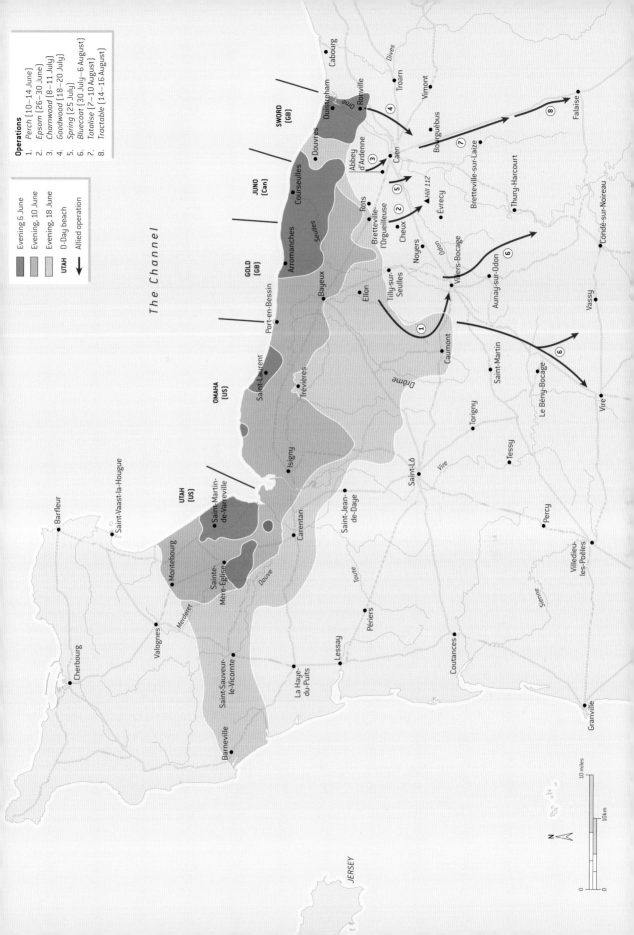

Operations

1. *Perch* (10–14 June)
2. *Epsom* (26–30 June)
3. *Charnwood* (8–11 July)
4. *Goodwood* (18–20 July)
5. *Spring* (25 July)
6. *Bluecoat* (30 July–6 August)
7. *Totalise* (7–10 August)
8. *Tractable* (14–16 August)

Evening 6 June
Evening 10 June
Evening 18 June
UTAH D-Day beach
Allied operation

The Channel

JERSEY

SWORD
(GB)

JUNO
(Can)

GOLD
(GB)

OMAHA
(US)

UTAH
(US)

Cabourg
Dives
Troarn
Vimont
Ouistreham
Ranville
Orne
Falaise
Douvres
Bourguébus
Abbey
d'Ardenne
Caen
Bretteville-sur-Laize
Courseulles
Thury-Harcourt
Seulles
Rots
Hill 112
Condé-sur-Noireau
Bretteville-
l'Orgueilleuse
Cheux
Évrecy
Arromanches
Nogers
Odon
Villers-Bocage
Aunay-sur-Odon
Vassy
Bayeux
Ellon
Tilly-sur-
Seulles
Port-en-Bessin
Drôme
Caumont
Saint-Martin
Le Bény-Bocage
Vire
Saint-Laurent
Trévières
Torigny
Tessy
Percy
Isigny
Vire
Saint-Lô
Villedieu-
les-Poêles
Saint-Martin-
de-Varreville
Carentan
Saint-Jean-
de-Daye
Barfleur
Saint-Vaast-la-Hougue
Montebourg
Douve
Sainte-
Mère-Église
Toute
Sienne
Granville
Valognes
Merderet
Coutances
Cherbourg
Saint-Sauveur-
le-Vicomte
Périers
Lessay
Barneville
La Haye-
du-Puits

N

10 miles

10km

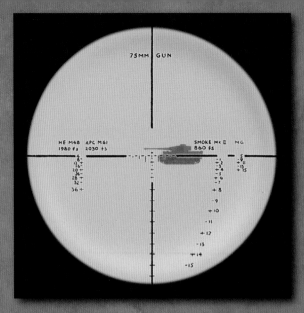

CHURCHILL GUNSIGHT NO. 50 VIEW

6-pdr Churchills were fitted with Telescope No. 39 sights, with 1.8x magnification, while 75mm tanks used the No. 50 illustrated here, with 1.9x or 3x magnification.

The elevation scales on the left allowed adjustment for range when firing 75mm HE or AP. Smoke rounds had much lower velocity, so guns had to be elevated more to achieve the same range using the scale on the right. The scale on the far right is for the coaxial machine gun.

75mm trajectories dropped significantly at longer ranges, so accurate estimation of range was vital. The 6-pdr's higher velocity gave it a flatter trajectory and made it less sensitive to poor range estimation – it would still hit with 200m error in the estimated range.

Infantry tanks were not invulnerable. The hedgerows channelled tanks, and gaps were often mined or covered by anti-tank guns, rarely spotted until they fired. Tanks could crash through hedges or try to climb them, but this exposed their vulnerable belly plates.

Commanders exposing themselves for better visibility often became casualties. However, if tanks stayed closed down, their limited vision ports and periscopes made them vulnerable to enemy infantry with bundle charges or Panzerfausts. (Panzerfausts and Panzershrecks accounted for only 6 per cent of Allied tank casualties in Normandy, simply because there were numerous other effective anti-tank weapons available; these casualties reached 34 per cent by the last months of the war when such weapons were extensively used for lack of anything better.)

The infantry spotted threats to tanks better than the tanks themselves, so working together for mutual survival was imperative. However, several factors hampered this.

Communication was an obvious problem. The noise inside tanks and their limited visibility made coordination via shouted or visual signals difficult. Tank and infantry units were not on the same radio net, though some vehicles had second sets on infantry frequencies. Even so, close terrain often blocked signals from infantry radios, they had limited battery lives and their operators were often killed by artillery or by snipers.

Climbing onto the turret to talk to the commander was risky for both infantryman and tank commander, exposing them to the numerous German snipers. Infantry tanks

were therefore fitted with telephones at the rear, for infantry to direct the tank's fire or speak with the commander without either party exposing themselves. However, there was no way for tank commanders to get an infantry officer's attention without getting out to look for him.

Doctrine and training was also problematic. Tanks were developed during World War I as infantry support weapons, but during the interwar period the Royal Tank Corps' vision of itself as a decisive independent arm meant it emphasized the armoured divisions over infantry support work. Equally, senior infantry officers rarely had experience of commanding armour or understood its limitations.

British Infantry Tank doctrine itself was rather confused. Montgomery disagreed with the official War Office doctrine, preferring methods evolved by Eighth Army, which relegated infantry to a supporting role. These worked well in North Africa, but were less suitable for very different European battlefields.

In the resulting confusion, units adopted whatever methods seemed best to them. This would have sufficed had infantry tanks been permanently attached to infantry units, so each knew what to expect from the other. However, Montgomery insisted all tank units should be interchangeable and able to operate in any armoured role, so Churchill units found themselves supporting infantry trained in very different methods with only a few days' practice together before going into battle.

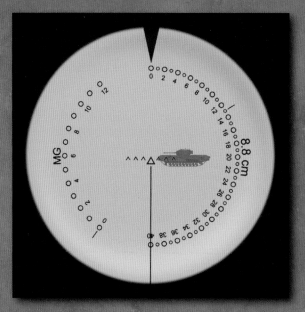

TIGER GUNSIGHT VIEW

Most Tigers used binocular TZF 9b Turmzeilfernrohr (turret telescopic sight) with 2.5x magnification and 25° field of view, so gunners effectively saw a triangle with its point on the lens and a base 444m wide at 1,000m. Vehicles built after March 1944 had the monocular TZF 9c instead, with 2.5x magnification for wide view or 5x for longer ranges.

The chevrons were used for stadiametric range estimation, though they were not always used in the heat of action. The small ones were two 'marks' (Stich) wide, and the large four. Each Stich was 1m wide on a target 1,000m

away, so if a target known to be 2m wide covered four Stich, the range was 500m, whereas if it covered one Stich, the range was 2,000m.

They also served to lead moving targets – the *Tigerfibel* advised leading three Stich per 10km of target speed for AP, or four for the slower HE.

The range scales round the outside were rotated until the estimated range aligned with the index mark – the right-hand scale was for the main 88mm gun and the left for the coaxial MG.

Unsurprisingly, the best results came when units were partnered with infantry they had previously trained with, such as 6th Guards Tank Brigade for Operation *Bluecoat*, but some infantry units had little chance to work with tanks before D-Day, and had to learn tank/infantry cooperation 'on the job'.

Despite these problems, Churchill units ultimately developed tactics for the bocage. Tanks fired HE rounds into likely positions from a distance, then half the tanks advanced across the field, spraying the far hedge-line with machine-gun fire while the other half remained stationary, watching for the flashes of enemy tanks or anti-tank guns firing. The overwatching tanks then moved forward while the accompanying infantry went through the hedge to clear out Panzerfausts and find gaps for the tanks, then the procedure was repeated for the next field.

It was vital that the tanks did not get too far ahead of the infantry. If this happened, the Germans would hold their fire and allow the tanks to pass through their positions. They could then suppress the following British infantry with machine guns, before exploiting the poor visibility of the unsupported tanks to pick them off from flanks and rear.

Infantry support was not only done by Churchills, as British production only supplied enough for three of the eight army tank brigades and the remainder were equipped with Shermans. With lighter armour, these often either tried to 'shoot in' infantry attacks from a distance, which was less effective, or tried to operate like Churchills and took heavier casualties.

Indeed, Montgomery's experience on the rather different battlefields of North Africa meant he supported ending Infantry Tank production (including the Churchill) in favour of a 'capital' or 'universal' tank similar to the Sherman. Sherman- and Cromwell-equipped armoured divisions were therefore used in assault or infantry support roles, despite their vehicles and training being less suitable.

OPERATION *JUPITER*, 10–11 JULY 1944

Churchills and Tigers rarely fought each other. A notable exception was during the Battle for Hill 112. Despite its modest height, this hill dominated routes to the open ground beyond Caen, providing excellent artillery observation points, and both sides recognized its importance. Hill 112 was actually captured by 11th Armoured Division during Operation *Epsom* (26–30 June), but German pressure forced elements of the division to withdraw.

Operation *Jupiter* saw 31st Tank Brigade attached to 43rd (Wessex) Infantry Division, which used two of its three infantry brigades in the initial attack, with the third held in reserve. The 129th Brigade, supported by 7 RTR, were to capture Hill 112 then form a defensive flank facing Évrecy. The 130th Brigade, supported by 9 RTR, were to capture Les Duanes and Château de Fontaine then take Éterville and Maltot and establish a defensive line between them. The 43rd Division's third (214th) Brigade and 4th Armoured Brigade would then advance between the 129th and 130th brigades to create a bridgehead over the Orne. The 46th (Highland) Brigade of 15th (Scottish) Division and 7 RTR's B squadron would then clear the ground between the Odon, the Orne and the western suburbs of Caen.

They were opposed by II.SS-Panzer-Korps, comprising 9.SS-Panzer-Division (Hohenstaufen) and 10.SS-Panzer-Division (Frundsberg). Each Panzer division included two three-battalion Panzergrenadier regiments – each roughly equivalent to British brigades – a tank regiment and various artillery, reconnaissance and engineer units. Divisional tank regiments theoretically had one battalion with PzKpfw IVs and StuGs and a second of Panthers, but 10.SS-Panzer-Division lacked its Panther battalion.

These Panzer divisions were transferred to Normandy to conduct a strategic counter-attack, but the pressure of Operation *Epsom* forced the Germans to feed them into the line piecemeal. Both divisions had taken losses during the *Epsom* battle, but were reinforced that morning by the Tigers of s.SS-Pz.Abt. 102.

The British artillery bombardment began at 0445hrs, just before dawn, using the combined artillery of four divisions, plus the medium and heavy guns of 3rd and 8th AGRAs (Army Group Royal Artillery) and naval gunnery, over 1,000 guns in total.

It far exceeded anything the SS had experienced on the Eastern Front, and suppressed the German units as the British advance began at 0500hrs. However, it also triggered German defensive artillery, inflicting the first casualties on the advancing British.

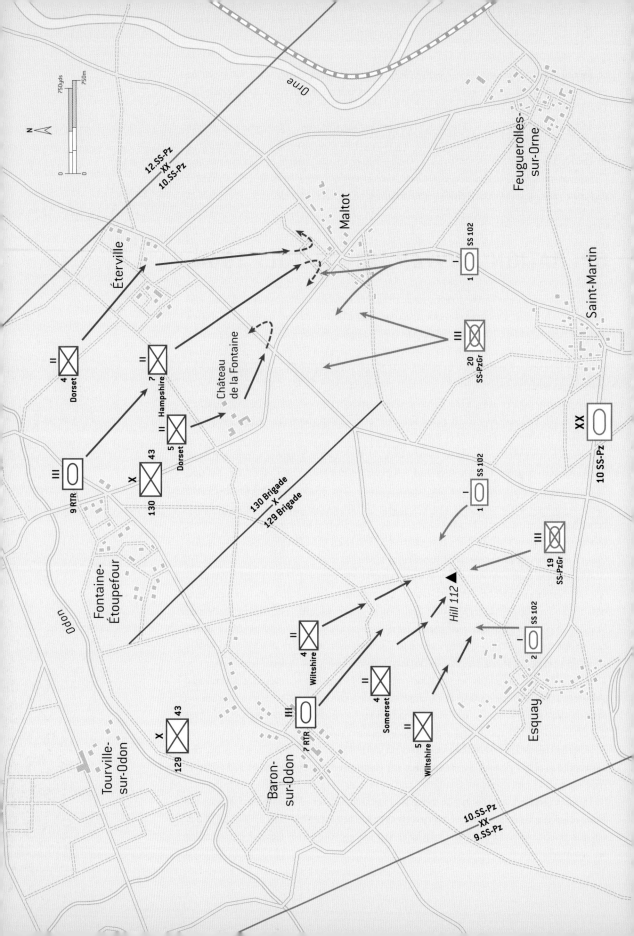

750yds
750m

N

12.SS-Pz
XX
10.SS-Pz

Orne

Maltot

Feuguerolles-
sur-Orne

SS 102
0
1 —

Saint-Martin

Éterville

III
XX
20
SS-PzGr

II
4
Dorset

II
7
Hampshire

Château
de la Fontaine

II
5
Dorset

X
43
130

III
0
9 RTR

130 Brigade
X
129 Brigade

XX
10 SS-Pz

SS 102
0
1 —

III
XX
19
SS-PzGr

Fontaine-
Étoupefour

Odon

Hill 112

SS 102
0
2 —

II
4
Wiltshire

III
0
7 RTR

II
4
Somerset

Esquay

X
43
129

Tourville-
sur-Odon

Baron-
sur-Odon

II
5
Wiltshire

10.SS-Pz
XX
9.SS-Pz

In the 130th Brigade sector, the 5th Bn Dorset Regiment, supported by Churchills from B Squadron 9 RTR, rapidly took the Les Duanes farm complex while the defenders were still stunned by the barrage. However, they had a much harder time clearing the Château de Fontaine and its outbuildings. This would be taken over by 7th Bn Somerset Light Infantry from 214th Brigade, while 5th Dorsets advanced to establish defensive positions along the Caen–Évrecy road.

Meanwhile, 4th Bn Dorset Regiment advanced on Éterville, led by Churchills of C Squadron and Crocodiles from 141 RAC, which engaged enemy machine-gun and anti-tank positions with HE and flame. However, the tanks were extremely vulnerable in the village itself, and it was cleared by infantry, who reported occupying Éterville by 0745hrs, though fighting there continued for the rest of the day, delaying the 4th Dorsets moving to reinforce 7th Bn Hampshire Regiment as they advanced towards Maltot.

C Squadron took up defensive positions covering the open flank, supported by M10 tank destroyers. However, the open-topped M10s were vulnerable to artillery, and several were knocked out.

The 129th Brigade had no villages to capture and advanced with all three battalions (4th Bn Wiltshire Regiment, 4th Bn Somerset Light Infantry and 5th Bn Wiltshire Regiment) in line, rather than the usual 'two forward, one in reserve', each supported by a squadron from 7 RTR. They were to clear the German infantry positions on Hill 112, establish artillery observation posts on the crest and set up defences on the rear slope.

They reached the crest despite significant casualties from artillery and machine-gun fire, but were counter-attacked by the seven operational Tiger tanks of s.SS-Pz.Abt. 102's 2.Kompanie. These were engaged by 4th Wiltshire's anti-tank platoon and 7 RTR Churchills, but the latter were clearly outgunned, despite reinforcement from a troop of M10s.

The 4th Somersets' line of advance was more exposed, and they also took heavy casualties. Several supporting Churchills were knocked out by PzKpfw IVs from 10. SS-Panzer-Division on Hill 112, though several of the panzers were also destroyed.

The Somersets dug in 400m short of the crest when more PzKpfw IVs counter-attacked on their flank. These were engaged by both the accompanying Churchills and the battalions' own 6-pdrs, though the latter's sights were blocked by the waist-high wheat.

The Somersets' advance stalled with three of their four company commanders already casualties, and they were struggling to hold the ground they had taken. The 7 RTR's C Squadron lost six tanks and retreated to less vulnerable hull-down positions. One Churchill (commanded by Corporal Sheldon) claimed to have destroyed three Tigers, though this is not supported by German records.

Alongside them, 5th Wiltshires ran into similar problems, and were also pinned down short of their objective and attacked by PzKpfw IVs, though they managed to destroy one with a PIAT.

Meanwhile, back with 130th Brigade, 7th Hampshires passed between the two Dorset battalions to take the village of Maltot, which they expected to be lightly held. Supporting tanks from 9 RTR's A Squadron occupied the surrounding orchards, and infantry were entering the village by 0835hrs, when a storm of fire erupted from

German infantry positions bypassed during the advance, from several tanks in Maltot itself and from a Tiger platoon of 1.Kompanie s.SS-Pz.Abt. 102 on Hill 112, using their long range to fire across the valley against the Churchills' thinner side armour.

A second platoon of Tigers moved around the village, arriving almost simultaneously with the British tanks, and rapidly knocked out a number of Churchills and M10s at close range.

Despite this, at 0915hrs, the 7th Hampshires signalled Brigade HQ they had taken Maltot, though in reality numerous German positions remained unsubdued in the village.

The 5th Dorsets attempted to move forward to support the Hampshires, but were forced back by fire from Tigers on Hill 112, which dominated the ground the Dorsets were trying to cross.

By 1035hrs, nine of the Churchills with the 7th Hampshires had been knocked out. The infantry were digging in and fighting off counter-attacks rather than advancing, and lost contact with Brigade HQ when their battalion HQ vehicles were destroyed. Meanwhile, German reinforcements had been dispatched to Maltot, including a Panzergrenadier regiment, the divisional reconnaissance battalion and a platoon of Tigers.

By 1200hrs, 9 RTR's A Squadron at Maltot had lost their commanding officer, and with only four operational tanks remaining they were forced to retreat, leaving the Hampshires without tank support. German infantry steadily recaptured positions within the village itself; while British air and artillery strikes slowed German reinforcements, they could not be used within the village itself without also hitting the British.

By 1300hrs, the British held Éterville and still had a foothold in Maltot, but the assault on Hill 112 had clearly stalled. The 4th Armoured Brigade, intended to exploit the breakthrough, was pressed to commit its lead regiment to support the attack. However, its commander refused, arguing that until the flanking fire of the Tigers on Hill 112 was suppressed, sending a regiment of Shermans forward would cost 75 per cent of its tanks and achieve nothing.

By 1500hrs, the division commander, Major-General Thomas, ordered 4th Dorsets forward to support the Hampshires in Maltot, and sent the division's last reserve, 5th Bn Duke of Cornwall's Light Infantry of 214th Brigade to reinforce the attack on Hill 112, since taking Maltot was impossible while the Germans there could enfilade any attacking force.

As 4th Dorsets reached Maltot, supported by the Churchills of C Squadron 7 RTR, they encountered the remaining Hampshires withdrawing from the village, having been driven out by the Germans, and several of their accompanying M10s were knocked out by artillery or Tigers.

By 1645hrs, 4th Dorsets had re-established a foothold in Maltot, but were unable to drive out the Germans. A battery of towed 17-pdr AT guns sent forward to form an anti-tank screen against the Tigers was overrun, while C Squadron fought an unequal tank battle, losing most of its vehicles.

By 2030hrs, the British forces in and around Maltot were given permission to withdraw. The Germans followed up and counter-attacked Éterville, now held by the 9th Cameronians and another battery of towed 17-pdrs, and breached the defensive perimeter. Fighting there continued into the night before the Germans were driven back.

Meanwhile, 5th Duke of Cornwall's, supported by A Squadron 7 RTR, reached the 4th Somerset's positions as an attack by German Panzergrenadiers and Tigers was broken up by artillery, and attacked at 2030hrs, trying to gain the hill crest 400yd ahead. By 2100hrs, they had reached the wood on the crest, where they were reinforced by a towed 17-pdr battery, but were counter-attacked by the remaining Tigers of s.SS-Pz.Abt. 102 and two companies of Panzergrenadiers. Though the attack was beaten off, the vulnerable anti-tank gun crews suffered heavily and most were put out of action. Several Churchills were also knocked out, and the rest forced to retreat to hull-down positions. However, the Tigers could not enter the wood and the Panzergrenadiers took heavy casualties doing so.

Unusually, fighting continued into the night here, too. The British tried to break up the repeated counter-attacks with artillery fire, but 5th Duke of Cornwall's were worn down and by 0300hrs the following morning, they requested permission to withdraw.

Just before dawn, a squadron of Shermans of the Scots Greys from 4th Armoured Division were sent to relieve pressure on the 5th Duke of Cornwall's. They destroyed several German outposts, but were clearly outgunned by the Tigers and quickly lost five Shermans and an OP tank before withdrawing. The fighting petered out, with the 5th Duke of Cornwall's finally withdrawing around 1500hrs the following day to avoid being overrun.

In retrospect, Operation *Jupiter*'s failure was entirely predictable, since it required British forces to push the numerically superior Germans out of prepared defensive positions, and that it achieved any success reflects the huge Allied superiority in artillery and air power.

Though a tactical victory for the Germans, who retained the vital ground, it was a strategic defeat, since the two irreplaceable Panzer divisions intended for strategic counter-attack were largely destroyed in the fighting.

The British kept up pressure on Hill 112, with Maltot finally falling on 22 July and the hill itself on 4 August.

The 31st Tank Brigade lost 39 Churchills in a single day of fighting, while s.SS-Pz. Abt. 102 lost six Tigers. The two German Panzer divisions also lost numerous tanks, so while the armoured exchange favoured the defending Germans, it was not completely one-sided.

The British 43rd Division took over 2,000 casualties in its first battle. German infantry casualties were around 4,180 for a two-week period including other fighting as well as Operation *Jupiter*.

RELIABILITY, RECOVERY AND REPAIR

The most powerful tank is only effective if it can get to the battlefield and be supported there. Equally, many 'knocked-out' tanks were not total losses, and good recovery and repair organizations could quickly return them to the fight.

The Tiger is often described as 'unreliable', and given numerous photographs of Tigers abandoned and blown up by their crews after breaking down, it is easy to see how it gained this reputation. However, the reality is more complicated.

The Tiger certainly had very short service intervals; according to the manual, it should be operated for only two hours or 10km before halting for refuelling and maintenance.

Many components had short operational lives partly because the engine and drive train were constantly running at near-maximum output to move a 56-ton tank rather than the 45-ton vehicle they were originally designed for, and partly because shortages forced use of inferior materials.

The Tiger's Maybach engine shared family commonality with other German tank engines and was designed for straightforward removal and replacement, but even so the high maintenance load required an entire workshop company for each battalion.

Multiple 18-ton SdKfz 9 FAMO half-tracks were required to tow a single Tiger, even on roads. The Germans lacked sufficiently powerful recovery vehicles, and most of those available were unarmoured. (Bundesarchiv, Bild 101I-022-2926-11A)

Each Tiger carried 534 litres of fuel. Even according to the manual, this was only enough for 140km by road or 80km cross-country. In practice consumption could be double this, especially when stationary vehicles kept engines running to power the turret traverse and radio. Refuelling was frequent, and each refill for a Tiger battalion's tanks required 15 trucks for fuel alone, plus a similar amount for its 200-odd supporting vehicles.

The sheer weight of Tigers created major problems. Germany had not invested in specialist recovery vehicles powerful enough to handle the Tiger, so recovery platoons used unarmoured SdKfz 9 18-ton half-tracks, originally built as artillery tractors by Fahrzeug- und Motorenbau GmbH (FAMO).

These had 270hp engines and a maximum towing weight of 28 tons, so at least two and often three were needed to tow a single disabled Tiger. Using one Tiger to recover another could be done for very short distances but was prohibited by regulations, since the vehicle itself was already underpowered and towing a second was likely to wreck the towing machine. The final organization for Tiger units supplemented the SdKfz 9s with three Bergepanthers, which at least had the same 700hp engine as the Tiger, but none of the units in Normandy received their full allocation in time for the campaign.

Once Tigers had been recovered, their weight required more special equipment. For example, the Olvar gearbox was a frequent source of problems, but replacing it required removal of the entire turret. This was too heavy for the 6-ton half-track cranes, and each workshop platoon in Tiger units was issued with a portable 16-ton gantry crane built by JS Fries, which could be disassembled and towed behind an SdKfz 9.

These problems were understood and accepted, since Tigers were intended as specialist breakthrough vehicles to smash holes in enemy defences for exploitation by other units while the Tigers received maintenance and were shipped by rail to wherever they were needed next.

Overall, with proper maintenance and support, Tigers were reasonably reliable vehicles. A study of average vehicle availability from May to December 1944 shows average availability of Tigers in the West was as high as the PzKpfw IV (both 73 per cent), and better than the Panther (71 per cent, once the early teething troubles were resolved) (Jentz 1997 p.11).

However, achieving these levels required significant maintenance, and doctrine emphasised Tiger units needed two to three weeks after operational use to restore them to full efficiency for further operations. Tigers were also to be delivered close to their objective by rail, to be deployed as entire units and to have adequate logistic support. None of these things were true in Normandy.

None of the Tiger units started the campaign close to the battlefront, and the railway system had been totally disrupted by the Allies. Since the Germans had no

Replacing Tiger gearboxes meant removing the entire turret using the portable Fries gantry crane ('Strabokrane') issued to each maintenance platoon, which folded for towing behind an SdKfz 9. (Bundesarchiv, Bild 101I-278-0875-33A)

road transporters capable of moving them, the Tigers faced far longer road movements on their own tracks than their designers envisaged.

This not only meant they suffered many breakdowns en route – two companies of s.SS-Pz.Abt. 101 arrived with only six and eight of their 14 tanks respectively after a six-day road march of 400km – but also meant the unit's vital recovery and repair assets were scattered over a long trail of broken-down vehicles leading to the front and were not immediately available to support vehicles actually going into combat.

Worse, Tiger battalions were often split up, which meant the specialist equipment of the workshop company could not support all the detached sub-units, which were unable to deal with major maintenance tasks or recover damaged vehicles.

A Churchill ARV Mk I fitted with a twin Bren AA mount in April 1943, with a Canadian Ram ARV in the background. (© Imperial War Museum, H 29358)

Finally, the Tiger units were short of spare parts and fuel. The spares shortage was a general problem, as Germany's desperate need for tanks forced them to maximize new vehicle production even when this meant limiting stocks of spares to support existing ones.

For example, HL230 engines had a typical life of 1,000–1,500km before requiring rebuilding. In 1943, around 25–30 per cent of production went as spares and replacements, which still only meant one spare engine for every three tanks. By the summer of 1944, this halved to only 15 per cent, then halved again to just 8 per cent by autumn 1944.

Many units found they needed several times the level of spares available to keep all their vehicles operational and were forced to cannibalize some damaged vehicles to fix others, or to destroy vehicles which could otherwise have been fixed.

Fuel was in equally short supply, since Germany lacked oil of her own and was dependent on its synthetic oil programme and on the Romanian oilfields. Both had been severely affected by Allied bombing – Romanian production had fallen 44 per cent by May 1944 – and her reserves were almost exhausted.

These shortages were worsened by the need to repair numerous breakdowns during the long and fuel-consuming road march to reach Normandy, then by air attack disrupting supply lines to the front.

The results were predicable, but disastrous: numerous Tigers were abandoned or destroyed by their crews because they could not be recovered or repaired, or even simply because they ran out of fuel.

Churchill units were in a much better position. The Churchill used a flat-12 engine to minimize vehicle height, which made it cramped and awkward to work on. However, its early problems were resolved by Normandy, and it was reasonably reliable.

Only Churchills with low mileages were used for the invasion, and were delivered almost to the battlefield by sea, so they began operations in excellent condition. Each Churchill squadron had an armoured recovery vehicle attached, capable of towing a disabled Churchill on its own, since it was both more powerful than the German SdKfz 9 and was recovering vehicles only two-thirds the weight of a Tiger.

Good Allied planning meant supplies of spare parts and fuel were plentiful and could reach the front without difficulty. Indeed, the Churchill units had 143 reserve tanks in the Forward Delivery Squadrons attached to each of the three brigades, or just over 25 per cent of front-line strength. They could thus remain at full strength despite vehicle losses, with some knocked-out crews returning to action the following day in new vehicles – something Tiger units could only dream of.

Each Churchill carried 150 gallons (682 litres) of fuel, giving a range of 127 miles/203km by road, or 60 miles/96km cross-country. Though never intended for long road marches, they proved surprisingly reliable during the rapid advance across France after the German collapse in Normandy, suffering relatively few mechanical breakdowns.

The Churchill ARV Mk II was fitted with a dummy gun turret containing a 25-ton recovery winch, increasing its capabilities. (© Imperial War Museum, KID 2482)

STATISTICS AND ANALYSIS

The Tiger and Churchill were designed for very different battlefield roles, so any fair comparison must focus on how well they achieved these.

The Tiger was designed as a breakthrough vehicle, but served mostly as a tank killer since it arrived as Germany was forced back onto the strategic defensive.

Judging its effectiveness is complicated by unreliable combat reports – enemy vehicles were often only briefly glimpsed, and Allied tankers were very prone to identify any tanks firing on them as 'Tigers'. Equally, gunners were not always certain they hit the tank fired at, and if so whether a shot penetrated or the vehicle had simply pulled back to a safer position.

The table below shows German tank losses based on unit records, but requires understanding of how these were completed. Germans units only classified tanks as losses if they could not be recovered, or were completely unrepairable – even gutted hulls awaiting shipment for factory rebuilding were not written off unit strength.

Table 3: Causes of reported Tiger losses by unit				
	s.SS-Pz.Abt. 101	s.SS-Pz.Abt. 102	s.Pz.Abt. 503	Total
Destroyed by direct or indirect fire	29	24	7	60
Destroyed or abandoned by crew	12	18	28	58
Destroyed by air attack	4	2	7	13
Returned to Germany for maintenance/repair	0	0	3	3
Totals	**45**	**44**	**45**	**134**

Of course, damaged vehicles often could be repaired. None of the 30 Tigers remaining to s.SS-Pz.Abt. 101 were still operational on 5 July 1944, but 21 returned to operational status over the following few days.

This meant units recorded very few losses early in the campaign when they were able to recover vehicles, no matter how badly damaged. They then recorded very high apparent losses during the last weeks of the campaign, when they were forced to abandon tanks already disabled earlier in the fighting but kept 'on the books' as theoretically repairable as well as those which broke down or ran out of fuel during the retreat.

Even strategic bombing was used to break German defences. This Tiger from 3.Kompanie, s.Pz.Abt. 503 was overturned by the Allied heavy bomber raid before Operation *Goodwood*, 18 July 1944, though two of its crew were rescued alive from inside. (© Imperial War Museum, B 8032)

By contrast, British units recorded losses as soon as tanks were damaged beyond the unit's own ability to repair and passed to REME units, which usually happened immediately even when tanks were clearly repairable and would return to action later.

Despite RAF claims, ground-attack aircraft accounted for only a small percentage of tank losses, though they destroyed numerous softskin vehicles. Meanwhile, as many German tanks were abandoned or destroyed by their crews as were destroyed in combat. However, as noted earlier, many of these may already have been combat-damaged before being destroyed, while only those completely destroyed or irrecoverable were credited to enemy fire directly.

Of course, how long tanks could fight before being knocked out was just as important. British analysis of battlefield wrecks indicated it took an average of 1.63 hits from German gunnery to knock out a Sherman, and a surprisingly low 1.2 Allied hits to knock out a PzKpfw IV. Meanwhile, it required 2.55 hits to deal with a Panther, and an impressive 4.2 hits to disable a Tiger.

The other side of the equation is how many Allied tanks were destroyed by Tigers, and the oft-quoted claim it took five Allied tanks to kill a Tiger. There are several things to remember here.

Firstly, most Allied tanks were not destroyed by their German equivalents. Even based on German kill claims for the first month of fighting (which obviously exclude tanks lost to mines, mechanical breakdown etc.), tanks only accounted for 227 (42 per cent) of the 537 British tank kills claimed, with the remainder being anti-tank guns, Jagdpanzers, artillery or infantry weapons.

Second, though the 5:1 ratio comes from popular post-war books rather than official contemporary analysis, it does not appear completely without foundation. For example, s.SS-Pz.Abt. 102 claimed to have destroyed 227 tanks, 28 anti-tank guns and 23 half-tracks or carriers during the Normandy campaign, while losing all but one of its 45 Tigers. Assuming we accept the kill claim at face value – which is not a given

– this gives a kill ratio of 5.16:1. (Eighteen of the battalion's Tigers – 40 per cent, a fairly typical figure – were abandoned or destroyed by their own crews. They have been included in the ratio above, as the claimed kills would also include British vehicles which were subsequently repaired.)

However, this may not say much about the relative quality of the tanks involved.

For one thing, other German AFVs achieved equally high kill ratios in Normandy – by 23 July, Allied tank losses totalled 2,395 tanks to 481 German tanks and assault guns, or around 5:1. Most of these were not caused by Tiger units, but all were achieved against Allied crews going into combat for the first time. These kill ratios then dropped off markedly during the later European fighting, as experienced German crews were killed and Allied crews became more experienced. This suggests the quality of the crew – rather than the tank – is a major factor, which fits with a similar decline in German kill ratios on the Eastern Front over the same period.

Post-war analysis also suggested the single most important factor in tank combat was not technical, but which tank spotted its opponent first, fired first and hit first. Since the Germans were on the defensive for much of the Normandy fighting, their tanks were often stationary and in cover. This gave them a massive advantage over Allied tanks advancing in the open, even if all else was equal.

Finally, Tigers took a great deal of time and resource to build, and Germany was less able to replace lost vehicles than the Allies. Each Tiger cost 400,000 Reichsmarks to produce, twice the price of a Panther which had equivalent front armour and a long 75mm gun with equal penetration to the Tiger's 88mm. Even more strikingly, it was four times the price of a StuG III, and perhaps Germany might have been better with larger numbers of cheaper but still effective tanks.

Ultimately, however effective the Tiger was as a tank, it required strong supply and support services, and by the end of the Normandy campaign, those were breaking down. Almost every Tiger committed to Normandy was lost – whether destroyed or

One of the last surviving Tigers at the Musée des Blindés, Saumur, with the single hole in its mantlet for the later monocular TZF 9c gunsight, single central headlight and Zimmerit anti-magnetic paste. It served in Normandy with s.SS-Pz.Abt. 102, then briefly with the Free French. (Craig Moore)

abandoned – and even where units were reconstituted later, they had lost most of their veterans, making them less effective.

By contrast, although 6-pdr APDS rounds made a proportion of Churchills surprisingly good tank killers, most 75mm versions were indifferent in tank-versus-tank engagements and could only penetrate a Tiger's armour at very close range, or by working around for flank or rear shots.

However, this misses the point, as the Normandy campaign saw the Churchill used in its intended role as an infantry support machine, which it did well.

In a primarily infantry battle – which the bocage fighting undoubtedly was – this was a critical role, as the infantry required both moral and physical support to achieve their aims.

Some 171 Churchills (roughly one-third of those deployed) were destroyed during the campaign, though the majority of these could be replaced from the immediate reserves within each tank brigade as this level of loss was only slightly above that envisaged during the planning.

Indeed, the British were willing to accept tank losses if it saved infantry, who were already bearing the brunt of casualties. The Churchill had a clear advantage over the lighter Sherman here – even the earlier versions had a roughly one-in-three chance of surviving a hit from an 88mm or the Panther's long 75mm, or better than 50/50 odds against the short 75mm L/48 fitted to PzKpfw IV or StuGs, and the up-armoured Mk VII was significantly better.

While failing to achieve the dramatic breakthrough Montgomery wanted, the infantry and their supporting tanks maintained continual pressure on the Germans, robbing them of the initiative and forcing them to commit their reserves piecemeal, including the precious Panzer divisions.

Indeed, while the tenacious German defence caused great difficulties, their commitment of so many troops ultimately worked to the Allies' advantage: once Normandy fell, the rest of France was liberated quickly and with much less fighting than originally expected.

Overall, Churchills were well protected and mobile, just within the weight limit for standard bridging equipment, and more importantly could be deployed and supported in numbers – each one cost £11,150, roughly 112,000 Reichsmarks or the cost of a PzKpfw IV.

While it was outgunned by many German tanks, it operated as part of larger forces that allowed the Allies to play to their strengths, notably their superiority in artillery and air power. While these might not necessarily destroy opposing tanks directly, the campaign showed how powerful tank units quickly lost fighting power when this superiority prevented them being supplied or maintained.

This fitted well into the overall Allied strategy of emphasizing weight of material rather than exceptional individual tanks, in the same way Britain did not embrace the concept of 'ace' tank commanders.

Such analysis should not forget the human cost of tank warfare. Though a great deal depended on circumstance, a good rule of thumb is that each tank knocked out meant one man killed and another seriously injured. In addition, about a third of the casualties tank units took were to men not in their tanks, inflicted by artillery and other causes.

CONCLUSION

In April 1944, the MP Richard Stokes – a former World War I officer and vociferous critic of British tank design – asked the government to put a Tiger and a Churchill on display for MPs to compare the two and judge for themselves whether his criticism of British tanks was correct. The government refused – perhaps sensibly, given the need to maintain morale – but on paper the Tiger was easily the better tank.

However, tanks are not 'Top Trumps' and there is more to armoured warfare than tables of armour thickness and gun penetration.

Neither vehicle was present in large numbers – there were only eight battalions of Churchill gun tanks in Normandy, and three of Tigers, making up less than 10 per cent of the tank strength on each side.

In the right circumstances, Tigers could have effects totally disproportionate to their numbers, as at Villers-Bocage where Michael Wittmann destroyed numerous British tanks and light vehicles, and more importantly blunted a British advance, buying time to organize proper defences.

On the other hand, despite German propaganda and the fear they aroused in Allied troops, Tigers were never invincible. The German army issued instructions to Tiger crews in September 1944 warning against overconfidence, and reminding them they could not ignore basic rules of armoured combat or the use of terrain because of their thick armour.

When such rules were ignored, the powerful weapons available by mid-1944 meant Tigers could be shockingly vulnerable. Wittmann was killed in Normandy leading six Tigers across open ground without reconnaissance. Five were destroyed in moments, without inflicting any casualties on their opponents.

The Tiger's unreliability has been overplayed, but it did require a great deal of support to keep it operational. Although they inflicted significant casualties on Allied tanks, the German logistic system was ultimately unable to support them with fuel and ammunition or meet their high maintenance load.

Once the front crumbled and the pocket closed around the German army, the Tigers were doomed. Most were destroyed by their own crews after they ran out of fuel, broke down or took damage that would have been repairable had adequate recovery vehicles been available – consequences of the endemic German over-emphasis on 'teeth' arms at the cost of things needed to support them.

By contrast, the Churchill was probably the most successful British tank of the war. It overcame its early mechanical problems, and could be produced in reasonably large numbers.

It carried as much armour as the Tiger, and indeed the Mk VII which appeared shortly before Normandy actually carried significantly more – an impressive achievement in a vehicle only two-thirds the weight of a Tiger.

British soldiers of the Durham Light Infantry inspect an abandoned Tiger from 3. Kompanie, s.SS-Pz.Abt. 101 during Operation *Epsom*, 28 June 1944. (© Imperial War Museum, B 6140)

The Churchill looked rather dated by the Normandy campaign, though the Mk VII was effectively a new design. It was one of the few British designs that was successfully upgraded, without suffering the problems of reduced turret crew that hampered other up-gunned British tanks such as the Valentine.

The Churchill's greatest weakness was that it was – in common with many British designs – somewhat under-gunned. In fairness, its primary role was infantry support rather than fighting other tanks and the 75mm was perfectly adequate for that. Meanwhile, APDS ammunition made the single 6-pdr Churchill in each troop a surprisingly good – and underrated – tank killer when it was available, almost equivalent to the famous Sherman Firefly but without the latter's various disadvantages.

It performed well in its designed role as an infantry-support vehicle, with the best example being the advance of 6 miles through the bocage in one day during Operation *Bluecoat*. However, operations in Normandy were hampered by crews who might be well trained individually but lacked combat experience, and by not working consistently with the same infantry units to build mutual confidence and standard procedures, so things had to be learned from scratch each time.

Overall, both ultimately represented 'dead end' design paths. The 90mm-armed US M26 Pershing – partly designed as a 'Tiger Tamer' – weighed in at only 46 tons, the same as the Panther, and while the US and Britain did build post-war heavy tanks – the M103 and Conqueror respectively – both were superseded by multi-role 'main battle tanks' that evolved from wartime medium designs.

Equally, the Churchill was Britain's last purpose-built infantry tank. Montgomery made no secret of his desire to see both infantry tanks and cruisers replaced by a single 'capital' or 'universal' tank usable in either role, and the next infantry tank design – the A43 Black Prince, effectively an enlarged 17-pdr-armed Churchill – was cancelled in favour of the Centurion Main Battle Tank.

BIBLIOGRAPHY

Agte, Patrick, *Michael Wittmann and The Waffen SS Tiger Commanders of the Leibstandarte in World War II* (Mechanicsburg, PA, Stackpole Books, 2006)

Anderson, Thomas, *Tiger* (Oxford, Osprey Publishing, 2013)

Beale, Peter, *Tank Tracks: 9th Battalion Royal Tank Regiment at War 1940–45* (Stroud, Alan Sutton Publishing, 1995)

Bernage, Georges, *The Panzers and the Battle of Normandy* (Bayeux, Editions Heimdal, 2000)

Buckley, John, *British Armour in the Normandy Campaign 1944* (Abingdon, Routledge, 2004)

DiNardo, R., *Germany's Panzer Arm in WWII* (Mechanicsburg, PA, Stackpole Books, 1997)

Dyson, Stephen, *Tank Twins; East End Brothers in Arms 1943–1945* (London, Leo Cooper, 1994)

Fletcher, David, *Tiger! The Tiger Tank: A British View* (London, HMSO, 1986)

Fletcher, David, *Mr Churchill's Tank: The British Infantry Tank Mark IV* (Atglen, PA, Schiffer Publishing, 1999)

Fletcher, David, *Churchill Infantry Tank* (Oxford, Osprey Publishing, 2019)

Foley, John, *Mailed Fist* (London, Panther Books, 1957)

Ford, Roger, *The Tiger Tank* (Staplehurst, Spellmount, 1998)

Forty, George, *Tiger Tank Battalions in World War II* (Minneapolis, MN, Zenith Press, 2008)

Gander, Terry J., *Tanks in Detail: PzKpfw VI Ausf E and B, Panzer VI Tiger I and II* (Hersham, Ian J. Allen, 2013)

Grant, Neil, *British Tank Crewman 1939–45* (Oxford, Osprey Publishing, 2017)

Greenwood, Trevor, *D-Day to Victory: The Diaries of a British Tank Commander* (London, Simon & Schuster 2012)

Gudgin, Peter, *The Tiger Tanks* (London, Arms & Armour Press, 1991)

Hayton, Mike, et al, *Tiger Tank: Panzerkampfwagen VI Tiger Ausf E (SdKFZ 181)*, (Yeovil, Haynes Publishing, 2011)

Jentz, Tom and Doyle, Hilary, *Tiger I Heavy Tank 1942–1945* (London, Osprey Publishing, 1993)

Jentz, Thomas L., *Panzer Truppen: The Complete Guide to the Creation and Combat Employment of Germany's Tank Force*, Vols I and II (Atglen, PA, Schiffer Publishing, 1996)

Jentz, Thomas L., *Germany's Tiger Tanks: Tiger I & II: Combat Tactics* (Atglen, PA, Schiffer Publishing, 1997)

Jentz, Thomas L. and Doyle, Hilary L., *Germany's Tiger Tanks: D.W. To Tiger 1: Design, Production & Modifications* (Atglen, PA, Schiffer Publishing, 2000)

Lochann, Dr Franz-Wilhelm, Rosen, Richard Freiherr von, and Rubbel, Alfred, *The Combat History of German Tiger Tank Battalion 503 in World War II* (Mechanicsburg, PA, Stackpole Books, 2008)

Montgomery, Nigel, *Churchill Tank 1941–56 (All Models)* (Yeovil, Haynes Publishing, 2013)

Napier, Stephen, *The Armoured Campaign in Normandy, June–August 1944* (Stroud, The History Press, 2017)

Perrett, Bryan, *The Churchill Tank* (London, Osprey Publishing, 1980)

Plant, John, *Infantry Tank Warfare* (London, New Generation Publishing, 2014)

Restayn, Jean, *Tiger I on the Western Front* (Paris, Histoire & Collections, 2001)

Rosen, Richard Freiherr Von, *Panzer Ace: The Memoirs of an Iron Cross Panzer Commander from Barbarossa to Normandy* (Barnsley, Greenhill Books, 2018)

Saunders, Tim, *Hill 112: Battles of the Odon – 1944* (Barnsley, Pen & Sword, 2001)

Schneider, Wolfgang, *Tigers in Normandy* (Barnsley, Pen & Sword, 2011)

Schneider, Wolfgang, *Tigers in Combat*, Vols I–III (Solihull, Helion & Co, 2000, 2005 and 2016)

Wilbeck, Christopher W., *Sledgehammers: The Strengths and Flaws of Tiger Tank Battalions in World War II* (Bedford, PA, Aberjona Press, 2004)

Williamson, Gordon, *Panzer Crewman 1939–45* (Oxford, Osprey Publishing, 2002)

INDEX

Page numbers in **bold** refer to illustration captions.